MAINS'S WOOIN'

A Drama of Northern Rural Life
with the original music

ABERDEEN CITY COUNCIL

ISBN 0-946920-14-1

FOREWORD

by Jack Webster

The reprinting of *Mains's Wooin'* in 1996 could not have found better timing. 1994 was the centenary year of Gavin Greig's popular rural saga, a play with music which not only reflects life in Aberdeenshire a hundred years ago but reminds us that much in human nature survives the superficial changes of time.

There was never a stage of my life when I was unaware of *Mains's Wooin'*. Gavin Greig was a playwright, a poet, a composer and an intellectual giant who gained an international reputation for his work as a folk-song collector.

As it happened, he was also my great-grandfather, a man who remained faithful to his rural roots and was equally at home with visiting professors and humble farm servants. There may have been something incongruous about such a man remaining as country dominie at Whitehill of New Deer when a much wider world was beckoning. But he didn't see it that way. It gave him a base for engaging his many talents in a variety of pursuits.

He died in middle-age, a delicate man distressed by the thought of the First World War which broke out in that same month of 1914. Throughout my childhood of the 1930s I was constantly reminded of such a famous man, revered as a scholar, loved as a human being.

My grandmother, Edith Greig, was the eldest of his nine children and she would paint for me a delightful picture of life at the Schoolhouse of Whitehill. With such a clutter of youngsters, it must have been hard for an artistic man to find the time and the peace to nurture his talent. But he was blessed with a wonderful wife in Granny Greig, everyone's favourite, who smoothed the domestic passage.

My grandmother would tell of the excitement as they prepared for the first production of *Mains's Wooin'* at New Deer in 1894. Chosen as the leading lady was the Buchan beauty of her day, Nellie Metcalfe, from the farm of Auchmunziel, New Deer (she would soon marry local farmer-cum-journalist Archie Campbell and give birth to their daughter Flora, later known as the distinguished poetess, Flora Garry).

What began as a local play, tailored to suit the community (dominie playing dominie, souter as souter etc) was soon spreading beyond Buchan, even beyond Scotland, as drama groups recognised a simple and unpretentious story which was universal. How else could it have survived for a hundred years?

I can still remember being carried home from many a village hall in the 1930s, long past my bedtime, because we had been representing the family at yet another performance of Grandpa Greig's play. (He was never anything but Grandpa Greig to us).

It took time for the significance of it all to dawn on me. By the Diamond Jubilee of *Mains's Wooin'* in 1954 I was already a journalist of twenty-three and more appreciative of the lady who took the chair on that memorable night – none other than the same Nellie Metcalfe who had graced the stage in 1894. She was still a beautiful woman, with the glint of youth in her eye.

Another milestone along the way was a remarkable production, set courageously out of doors on the Banffshire coast in 1963, when a gigantic cast including massed choirs and orchestra gave *Mains's Wooin'* its most spectacular airing.

Happily, my grandmother lived to see all that, indeed surviving into her nineties as the last of Gavin Greig's children, having gone from a world without a motor car to the first landing on the Moon, which happened weeks before her death in 1969.

With the decline of spoken Scots, there were always gloomy predictions for works like *Mains's Wooin'*. Robert Louis Stevenson once forecast an end for dialects within his own lifetime.

Sadly he died as a young man – in the year when *Mains's Wooin'* first hit the footlights. But even if he had lived for another hundred years, Stevenson's pessimism would still have been misplaced. Even in an age when our lowland language is under far greater attack from outside influence, There is still a place for authentic cultural expression like *Mains's Wooin'*. Long may it remain so.

As a descendant of Gavin Greig I'm delighted. I also suspect that in distant heavenly places they are holding a celebration, the dominie himself proposing a toast to the greater survival of rural life in his beloved Scotland.

EDITOR'S NOTES

When Gavin Greig took over the post of Schoolmaster at Whitehill School, New Deer, in the heart of the Buchan countryside in 1879, he soon threw himself into the local musical life. He ran small orchestras, choirs and brass bands, and played the organ in the churches and the piano on any number of social occasions. Before long he became more ambitious and attempted modest musical dramas such as *Bruce: an opera for juveniles, Queen Mary and Rizzio,* and *The Seasons and the Hours.* In 1892, furthermore, he achieved a rousing success with his musical *Prince Charlie,* with costumes hired from London for the large cast of over seventy, and a special train laid on for the Peterhead premiere.

But he was determined to write a work for and about the local people and their lives, to be 'the first attempt at native drama in which scene, character, speech and song are all direct and faithful reproductions.' From this came *Mains's Wooin'* and its first performances at New Deer on 3,4 and 6 April 1894 'broke all the records of public entertainment.' It was written closely around his local performers, and was altered as rehearsals proceeded to suit the abilities and characters of such friends as his schoolmaster colleague, Adam Dunbar, the first and most famous performer to play the central character, 'Mains of Bungray'.

It was subtitled *A Drama of Northern Rural Life* and was written in the Buchan speech (the Doric). There are exceptions – English is used either by authority figures such as the Laird and his Page, the Policeman and the Gamekeeper (Greig did not hesitate to take off himself in the character of the Schoolmaster who employs the most high-falutin English of all), or the baddies, the Poachers who not only speak English, but Cockney at that. The cast of seventeen, furthermore, could be enlarged at will to include any number of 'youths and maids, harvesters, scholars' and the like, and the Harvest Home scene in Act 2 had a 'Procession of the Seasons' in which any number of children and adults could take part (and from newspaper reports it seems as though the entire population of New Deer crossed the stage at one point or another).

v

Although Greig went on to write another grand musical in *Robbie Burns* the following year, it did not have the same success. In 1896 or 1897 he wrote *Main's Again, A sequel to "Main's Wooin'"; A Drama of Northern Rural Life with Music.* Although this is perhaps the funniest play ever written in Scots, it had a small cast, the music was only a song at the beginning and end, and it never was the same success as *Mains's Wooin'*.

For *Mains's Wooin'* was not only a runaway success at the time, it went on to become 'the North-East's equivalent of the Oberammergau Passion Play', and has practically never been out of performance since. The full musical score appears to have gone missing around the 1930s, however, and had to be guessed at thereafter. Most fortunately it was recently rediscovered by Victor Coutts, whose father George (brother of a son-in-law of Greig's) had obtained it from the famous Dufton Scott – who used to hold the copyright – for a performance in Buckie in 1928, and fortunately for us forgot to return it. For the first time for many years it has been possible to bring the words and music together again – hence this present edition.

Mains's Wooin' is a very clever mixture of local Scots life and operetta, appealing to both those who hankered for the old way of life that was rapidly vanishing by the end of the century, as well as to those who were striving to become more 'modern' and cultured. Interestingly enough, only two of the twenty-odd musical pieces are local folksong – 'The Bonnie Lass o' Fyvie' and 'Johnnie Sangster' (and Greig gives arrangements for these). The rest are mainly Greig's own compositions with a few songs from Burns.

An obvious explanation for this is that although Greig (along with the Reverend James Bruce Duncan of Weetingshill and Lynturk) is now world famous for the amazing collection of some 3,500 folksongs made in the North East before the First World War, (and now being published in eight superb volumes by Aberdeen and Edinburgh Universities as *The Greig-Duncan Folk Song Collection*) he did not, in fact, take up collecting local songs until 1903 or 1904. Before that – and this included the time of writing this play in 1896 – as a daughter once said: 'frankly, he knew nothing about them', and this is reflected in the music of *Mains's Wooin'*.

The other side of the coin is that we now have an excellent example of a late Victorian operetta, whose music was mainly Greig's own. Combined with his dramatic skills, careful observations of the way of life around him, and his sure handling of the Doric, this has resulted in a dramatic gem whose shine has never (and may never) become worn off.

Notes on the text

1. Greig's original 'NOTE' of introduction makes two main points: firstly, producers should not hesitate to adapt the play to local conditions such as size of hall, size and skills of available cast (Greig himself would do this freely) and secondly, *the performers' own local dialect should be used.*

The original 'NOTE' also referred to terms and conditions for public performances. These no longer apply and the play can be performed freely.

2. Page 7. Peter's last speech. 'Ye knicht in knickers' might best be altered to 'ye knicht in knickerbockers' if a cheap laugh is to be avoided from present day audiences.

3. Page 27. Substitute for 'Aberdeen' the nearest town with a Sheriff Court.

4. Page 31. The Dominie's gift of £5. This is meant to represent a very large sum indeed (it was the half-year fee for a female farm servant, for example). Make this sum more realistic for the present day.

5. Page 40. 'Peershoose' is the Poorhouse.

6. Page 57. 'Twenty Pounds' to buy out the Shepherd is an enormous sum in present day terms – around £3,500 in 1994. Make it up to a suitable figure to show Mains's extreme generosity.

Notes on on the music score

The surviving music is in Greig's own handwriting (although there are a few later additions in another hand). The score we have is for the PIANO for this was often all that Greig used, but it gives a firm basis for scoring for additional instruments.

It covers 'Hame and Guid-nicht' (page 5), 'Lads and Lasses to the Fair' (pages 13/14), 'The Bonnie Lass o' Fyvie' (pages 14/15), 'Heavenly Power' (page 22), 'Sleep my own, my loved one' (page 26), and 'Fare-thee-well' (page 27), 'Guid-Nicht and joy' (page 33), 'It's oh for the good old days' (pages 34/35), 'Johnnie Sangster' (pages 43/44), and 'Lord of the Seasons' (page 50).

[In addition to this score a photocopy of a *Mains's Wooin'* selection in Greig's handwriting is added. Part of the title has been lost.]

Page 11. 'I'm ower young to mairry yet' and 'My love she's but a lassie yet' are two well-known Burns' airs.

Page 12/13. 'Will ye gang to Mains o' Bungry, Maggie Anderson?'. Greig has supplied the sol-fa for this well-known tune.

Page 17. I cannot trace this single line, 'Mirk and rainy is the nicht'.

Page 22. 'It's a' for want o' pocket-money'. Untraced.

Page 38. 'Aye waukin' O'; a well-known song by Burns.

Page 43. 'Now's the day, and now's the hour'; well-known traditional tune used for 'Scots wha hae' and other songs.

Page 52/3. 'Maid with the golden hair' has sol-fa provided in the text. Greig also provides a piano accompaniment.

MAINS'S WOOIN"

A DRAMA

OF NORTHERN RURAL LIFE
WITH MUSIC.

BY

GAVIN GREIG

PRICE   One Shilling.

ABERDEEN:

D. WYLLIE & SON.

1912.

NOTE.

A S the resources of the amateur stage, for which the following play is intended, vary in different places, it has been judged best to give the stage directions in pretty general terms. A capable stage manager will easily make the necessary adaptations in each case. It is also recommended that the pronunciation of the vernacular, varying, as it does, more or less, with the locality, be assimilated to that of the district where the play happens to be produced.

The Procession of the Seasons, in the final scene, may, if it is deemed advisable, be omitted, and a Dance, or some other kind of Exhibition, be substituted for it. If this is done, certain slight changes will fall to be made in the context. It is advised, however, that, in any case, the Thanksgiving Chorus, "Lord of the Seasons," be retained.

For terms and conditions of public performance, application should be made to the Publishers.

CHARACTERS.

MAINS (*Well-to-do Farmer—middle-aged*).

PETER (*Mains's Man*).

SHEPHERD.

SOUTER.

JOHN ANDERSON (*Small Farmer—old*).

LAIRD.

DOMINIE (*Elderly*)

POLICEMAN.

GAMEKEEPER

SERGEANT.

POACHERS.

PAGE.

Mrs ANDERSON (*Middle-aged*).

MAGGIE }
JEANNIE } (*Daughters*).

HOUSEKEEPER.

OLD WOMAN (*May be played by Male*).

YOUTHS & MAIDENS.   HARVESTERS.   PIPER
    SCHOLARS

For the Procession of the Seasons.

TIME.

SPRING }
SUMMER } (*Ladies*).
AUTUMN }

HOURS (*Girls*).

QUARTETTE OF HERALDS.

MAINS'S WOOIN.'

ACT I.

SCENE I.—THE BRAES. SUNSET.

Picnic Company ready to return home. Picturesque grouping— ladies and girls in front, decked with flowers and greenery.

Chorus—Hame and Guid-nicht.

Far ayont Benachie see the red skies o' gloamin'
Hae blawn like a rose and are fadin' awa';
The day it is deen, and the evenin' is comin';
  It's hame and guid-nicht noo for ane and for a'.
  It's hame and guid-nicht, it's hame and guid-nicht,
  It's hame and guid-nicht noo for ane and for a'.

Tho' our joys like the hours be aye fadin' and fleetin',
Yet aften shall memory the vision reca',
And hope dream o' mony anither blithe meetin',—
  It's hame and guid-nicht noo for ane and for a'.
  It's hame and guid-nicht, it's hame and guid-nicht,
  It's hame and guid-nicht noo for ane and for a'.

Enter Mains.

Mains—Weel, lads and lasses, ye've jist been haein' a bit sang afore ye start for hame. It mak's a fine finish to the day's proceedin's. The cairts are yokin', and we'll hae to be movin'; but I see the laird comin' daun'rin' doon the walk, and we'll need to gie him three cheers afore we gang.

Dominie—Excuse me, Mr Sangster, but don't you think we should express our sense of indebtedness to our—ah—worthy proprietor in a more—ah—dignified and impressive manner? Might we not move a formal vote of thanks to Sir James?

Mains—Weel than, Dominie, ye can dee't yersel'. Ye've maist gift o' the gab, ye ken.

Dominie—Well—I have no objection to be the mouth-piece of this happy ·and—ah—distinguished company.

Enter Laird.

Laird—Good evening, ladies and gentlemen.

Mains—Good evenin', Sir Jeems.

Dominie—(*clearing his throat*) Sir James the Rose,—A very pleasant duty devolves on me on this —ah—auspicious and festive occasion. Through your beneficent kindness, Sir James, it has been permitted us to perambulate those picturesque and—ah—

delectable amenities, with their umbrageous and sequestered retreats—their—ah—so to speak, romantically sylvan—ah—ah— holes and corners,—qua pinus ingens albaque populus umbram hospitalem consociare amant ramis.

[Souter—(*aside*) Preserve's a', fat's that?]

In such environment, I say, it has been our privilege to spend this—ah—auspicious day with—ah—

Peter—(*shouting without*) Hi!

Dominie—Yes, high, very high delight on the part of—ah—

Peter—(*without and approaching*) Hi, lads and lasses!

Dominie—Yes, lads and lasses both; and—ah—

Peter—(*entering*) Fat are ye scutterin' aboot here for a' nicht? The cairts is yokit.

Mains—Peter, man, weesht man! Ye're interruptin' the proceedin's.

Peter—Oh, I didna ken. (*Aside to* Souter) Fat's adee wi' the Dominie?

Souter—He's swallowed the dictionar'. min, an's tryin' to get 'er aff o's stammack.

Laird—(*as* Dominie *is clearing his throat to resume his speech*) Yes, that's all right, Mr Thomson. I'm glad you have enjoyed yourselves. I hope you'll have a safe and pleasant journey home, and we shall be pleased to see you all back again next season, "When summer days have decked anew the flowery Braes."

Dominie—Three cheers for Sir James!

Company cheer. Exit Laird, *bowing.*

Mains—(*to Piper*) Noo, Piper, strik' up and lat's awa'.

Piper strikes up and marches round the stage and off— company following.

Shepherd—(*lingering behind and alone*) I hope Maggie will manage to get redd o' the company.

Souter—(*looking in from side*) Come on, Shepherd; they're jist startin'.

Shepherd—Oh, never mind me. I think I'll traivel a bit. It's a fine nicht, and I'll enjoy the walk.

Souter—Wi' guid company, nae doot, ye rogue. But please yersel'; (*disappearing*) I'm awa'.

Cheers heard without.

Shepherd—That's them aff at last*! Joy gae wi' them if they leave Maggie!—Oh I hope she's hingin' aboot.

Exit Shepherd. *Enter* Mains.

Mains—Ay, ay; I won'er if there's onybody left ahin' that I could gie a lift till in my gig. I mentioned it afore to Maggie

An'erson, and maybe she's wytin' aboot for me. I didna see her aboot the cairts onywye.

Enter MAGGIE, *but, seeing* MAINS, *is about to withdraw.*

Oh, come awa', Maggie, lass! I wis jist lookin' for ye. Isn't it lucky we've met?

MAGGIE—Oh, jist as folk think, Mains.

MAINS—Come noo, Maggie lass, be ceevil; for ye ken——it's —Come under my plaidie, the nicht's gaun to fa'—ye ken?

MAGGIE—Ay, I ken; but it's—Gae 'wa' wi' your plaidie, auld Donald, gae 'wa': I carena the cauld——

MAINS—Weesht, wumman, and nane o' your impudence! I'm nae an auld Donald. There's plenty bachelors as auld's me.

PETER—(*entering hastily*) Ay, there maybe *is* men as auld's you; but at this hoor o' the nicht they're sittin' at the cheek o' the fire wi' nichtkeps on and hostin' up the lum, nae gaun gallavantin' at picnics, offerin' to coort young lasses.—Come awa' hame, min, the gig's yokit!

MAINS—Peter, min, man Peter! Fat on earth, Peter man-- are ye deein' here?

PETER—Come awa' hame, ye auld feel, and nae haud folk lauchin' at ye.

MAINS—(*to* MAGGIE *who is moving off*) Maggie, lass, dinna gang awa'. Never mind Peter. (*To* PETER) Peter man, jist ye ca canny, man. Is't you or me that's maister, Peter man?

PETER—O weel, ye're maybe maister in a wye; but I wid like to ken fa's to be *mistress* at Mains o' Bungry. Gin ye can licht on ony dacent sensible wumman o' your ain age I'm nae jist carin' sae muckle. But (*pointing to* MAGGIE) daur ye to bring hame ony o' thae young senseless jauds to be mistress at *oor* toon!

MAGGIE (*tossing her head*) Dinna distress yersel, Peter man. I've nae intention o' comin' to Mains o' Bungry as mistress or servant either.

PETER (*imitating her movements and tone of voice*) Oh na! ye'll be on for some young glaiket chiel, wi' a heid as teem's shillin sids, and claes that the tylor hisna been peyed for, and likely never will.—Oh na!

MAINS—Ay, and here I believe is the very birkie comin'. I thocht there wis maybe some Johnnie in the bizzness.

Enter SHEPHERD.

I'm gaun to meet Johnnie, he's young and he's bonnie,
He's been at the picnic fu' trig and fu' braw.

SHEPHERD—None of your insolence, sir! (*crossing to* MAGGIE).

PETER—Nane o' yours, young herdie! (*Looking the* SHEPHERD *up and down*) Ye knicht in knickers, ye hero in hamespun! Gin ye daur to speak yon wye again to your betters, I'll——

SHEPHERD—(*turning on* PETER) Ye'll what? (*Squaring*) Ay, baith o' ye, gin ye like!

MAINS—(*seizing* PETER'S arm) Na, Peter, min! Nae fechtin' here! Gin ye shed the billie's bleed the laird'll be pullin' ye up for spilin' 's girse.

MAGGIE—(*taking* SHEPHERD'S *arm*) Come, awa', Johnnie: they're nae worth min'in'. Come on!

SHEPHERD—(*yielding*) I suppose ye're richt, Maggie—they're nae worth min'in'.

MAINS—Nae worth min'in'! By my saul!

PETER—(*following* SHEPHERD) Ay, ye'll as weel edge awa. Gin't hidna been for the lassie's sake,——

SHEPHERD—(*looking round*) Ay, gin't hidna been that!——

Exeunt SHEPHERD *and* MAGGIE.

MAINS—Never min' them, Peter. Jist lat them gang.

PETER—Ay, but I'll hae't oot wi' 'im yet, or my name's nae Peter Riddel.—(*Exit.*)

MAINS—(*alone*) Queer chap Peter. Nae sic an ill breet aifter'n a'.—Gran' servant: couldna dee wantin' 'im. He orders me aboot like ony bairn; but daur ony ither body to mint a word against me, and Peter is up in airms that vera instant—Queer chap Peter. . . . . . Weel, weel, I suppose I'll jist need to submit and gang hame my lane, though I'm awfu' mad to lat yon shepherd chiel get the better o' me and gang aff wi' Maggie. But I'll be upsides doon wi' 'im yet. Wyte till ye see.

Exit MAINS.

[END OF SCENE I.]

———◇———

SCENE II.—THE SOUTER'S SHOP.　MORNING.

SOUTER *seated on his stool at work. Sings some local folk-song, keeping time with his work.*

Enter TWO POACHERS.

1st POACHER—Well, shoemaker, can you do anything with a poor fellow's boot?

SOUTER—It depends. Lat's see't aff, and I'll tell ye.

POACHER *sits down on form and takes off boot. His toe appears through hole in stocking.*

I'm gled to see your big tae's some better.

2nd POACHER *laughs.*

1st POACHER—My toe better? How?

SOUTER—Weel than, it's lookin' oot.

1st POACHER—Never mind the toe; what about the boot?

SOUTER—(*examining boot*) Ye'd picket this ane up at the back o' a dyke; but there's nae sayin'—if it hid a new sole and new uppers, the pints micht maybe dee: *they're* nae jist a' thegither deen yet.

1st POACHER—You're mighty clever, Mr Snob; but wouldn't less do good?

SOUTER—Oh, I suppose I could ca in a curn tackets, maybe. The beet micht maybe stand that—wi' carefu' handlin', like.

1st POACHER—Well, just do that, and look sharp.

SOUTER *begins to drive tackets.*

SOUTER—Ay, ay, men, and ye'll be strangers in this locality?

2nd POACHER—Well, we ain't exactly residenters.

SOUTER—And faur micht ye come fae, maybe?

2nd POACHER—From home, of course.

SOUTER—(*always working as he talks*) I see; and ye'll be on the hunt—for wark—or maybe hares?

2nd POACHER—Man, shoemaker, if folk got paid for asking impudent questions you'd have retired with your fortune *long ago.*

SOUTER—And if folk wis ta'en up for their ill looks you twa billies wid 'a been in Peterheid LONG AGO.

1st POACHER—Hand me my boot, you ill-tongued rascal, and let's away!

SOUTER—(*throwing boot to him*) Hae! and that's fowerpence.

POACHER *puts on boot.*

1st POACHER—(*throwing threepence to* SOUTER *and marching out with his companion*) Ta, ta, Rossetty Ends!

SOUTER—(*collecting and counting the pennies*) Hi! ye want a penny!

1st POACHER—(*disappearing*) No, it's you that wants't! Ha! ha!

SOUTER—Sorra care! lat him gang.—(*Taking a cloth and wiping form on which* POACHERS *have been sitting*) They're a pair o' orra scoots, and I'll wager they're aifter some ill—poachin', stealin' hens, or maybe something waur; but, gin yon ill-faur'd billie leaves fit-marks ony wye ahin' him, I think I'll maybe manage to identifee them.—Weel, weel.—(*Resumes work*).

Enter SHEPHERD.

SHEPHERD—Ay, ay, Souter, and ye're aye stickin' in?

SOUTER—Ay, of coorse, a sooter aye sticks in to the *last.*

SHEPHERD—(*laughing*) I'm gled to fin' ye sae cheery in thae dull times.

SOUTER—And fa wid be cheery if a souter wisna?

SHEPHERD—And fat gies him ony advantage?

SOUTER—Weel, gin ye wis to loss your all, fat wid happen?

SHEPHERD—Oh, I suppose I wid jist be ruined.

SOUTER—Surely; but if I wis to loss *my awl* (*holding it up*)
I wid jist buy anither. They only cost thrippence.

SHEPHERD—Oh, souter man, that'll dee.—By-the-bye, wid ye-
hae onything gaun up the wye o'—o'—Knoweheid, maybe?

SOUTER—Ay, there's a pair o' beets o' Maggie An'erson's,
here that I've been solin'. They micht gang to Knowheid if
they'd feet in them.

SHEPHERD—But couldna they—be carriet?

SOUTER—Sae they likely will; but foo are ye spierin'?

SHEPHERD—Ah weel, ye see, I wis maybe to be—takin' a turn
roon—that wye the nicht—mysel—maybe like—ye ken; and I jist
thocht, ye see, aifter I come hame fae the Fair—I micht, maybe,
ye ken—like——

SOUTER—(*waving his hand and smiling*) It's a' richt, man.
I see the thing fine. Ye're jist wantin' an eeran' owre to see
Maggie.

SHEPHERD—Weel, maybe I am.

SOUTER—It's a' richt, man. I sympatheese wi' ye; for she's
a fine lass, Maggie; and atween you and me she ocht to be rale
weel suited.

SHEPHERD—Fat wye?

SOUTER—Weel, ye see (*taking one of the boots and tapping
the sole*) I'm a souter for her sole, and ye're a suitor for her
hert and hand—see?

SHEPHERD—O Souter man, that's waur and waur.—Gie's the
beets and lat's awa'.

SOUTER wraps boots in paper.

SOUTER—(*handing parcel to* SHEPHERD) Hae, man; and luck
gae wi' ye!

SHEPHERD—Thank ye, Souter, and guid-day.

SOUTER—Guid-day, Shepherd.

Exit SHEPHERD.

Ay, ay; and the Shepherd's owre heid and lugs wi' Maggie.
That's plain eneuch. I only wis' I may succeed as weel wi' her
sister Jeannie. Terrible thing love!——

O love, love, love; love it is a dizziness,
It winna lat a puir body gang aboot his bizziness.

Enter JEANNIE.

SOUTER rises to his feet.

O Jeannie lass, and that's you? Come awa' in by. I'm awfu'
gled to see your bonnie face. I wis jist mindin' on ye.

JEANNIE—Nane o' your impudence noo, Souter!

SOUTER—It's nae meant for impudence, I can assure ye.
Fat can I dee for ye?

Jeannie—Is my sister's boots ready?

Souter—Ye're a post ahin',—they're awa'.

Jeannie—Awa! Hoo can that be, and me cam' ance-eeran' for them?

Souter—Yon shepherd chiel, Jock Meerison, took them awa' wi' 'im.

Jeannie—Jock Meerison? Fat bizzness hid he?

Souter—Spier at 'im. I'm thinkin' he'll be wantin' an eeran' owre to see you.

Jeannie—Me? Na, na. It's Maggie, if it's onybody.

Souter—And dis naebody come to see you?

Jeannie—Na, na. (*Sings or says*)—

> For I'm owre young, I'm owre young,
> I'm owre young to mairry yet;
> I'm owre young, 'twad be a sin
> To tak' me frae my mammy yet.

Souter—Weel, weel, that's a pity, Jeannie lass, for I wis thinkin' o' comin' owre some nicht to see ye mysel'.

Jeannie—O weel, ye can jist come owre and see the auld folk.

Souter—Maybe the nicht?

Jeannie—Ay, gin ye like. They'll be at hame the nicht I think.

Souter—(*slyly*) And maybe ye'll be at hame yersel' tee?

Jeannie—Maybe I will; but I maun rin the noo.—Sae guid-day to ye, Souter.

Souter—Guid-day, Jeannie lass; and mind—the nicht!

Exit Jeannie.

(*Resuming work and singing*)—

> My love she's but a lassie yet,
> My love she's but a lassie yet,
> I'll lat her stand a year or twa,
> She'll nae be half sae saucy yet.

Enter Mains.

Mains—Guid-day, Souter; ye're jist haein' a bit sang to yersel' b' wye?

Souter—Jist that, Mains. Ye'll be on your wye to the Fair?

Mains—O fairly; and I thocht I wid come roon this wye and cry in a meenit in passin'.—I'm on the ootlook for a hoosekeeper. Ye dinna ken o' ony suitable wumman, d' ye, Souter?

Souter—Ach, man! The best hoosekeeper for you's a wife.

Mains—That's a' very guid, man. But ye see the lasses I wid like winna hae me. I've a big fairm and plenty siller; and yet some o' thae young jauds wid tak' a young coof o' a chiel

withoot a penny in his pouch afore the like o' me.—Souter, man,
you that's a gey knowin' kin' o' chap, fat micht the rizzen be?

SOUTER—Weel, Mains, ye see ye maybe dinna jist gang aboot
the thing in the richt wye, ye ken. Ye'll be owre prosaic and
maitter-o'-fac' kin'. Young chaps are fu' o' sentiment, and that
suits young lasses.—For instance, there's that chiel o' a shepherd,
Jock Meerison, when he gangs to coort Maggie An'erson——

MAINS—Dis *he* gang aifter Maggie?

SOUTER—Of coorse ye ken that. Ye min' the picnic?

MAINS—(*shaking fist*) The scoon'rel!

SOUTER—Weel, ye see he's a bonnie singer the Shepherd, and
wid sing serenades to Maggie, ye see.

MAINS—And couldna I dee that tee? I'm maybe nae jist
muckle o' a musicianer, but I can manage French, for instance,
rale weel.

SOUTER—But it's only *Scotch* Maggie could understand.

MAINS—Ye gowk! it's the *teen* French I mean.

SOUTER—Oh, I see. But that's nae eese, man. Ye couldna
weel sing a Psalm at a young lady's window on a Saiterday nicht.
Ye maun get up some *love* sang.

MAINS—For instance, than?

SOUTER—(*reflecting*) Weel—lat's see—there's (*scratching his
head with awl*) ay, there's "Will ye gang to the Hielans, Leezie
Lindsay?" Ye could cheenge't intil "Will ye gang to Mains o'
Bungry, Maggie An'erson?"

MAINS—Capital! Man, Souter, ye're a jainus! And hoo dis
the teen gang? I'll seen learn 'er.

SOUTER—Something like this,—(*sings*).

s₁.,l₁	d :-.r: m.f	s : m : r.m	r.,d : d
Will ye	gang to Mains o'	Bungry, Maggie	Anderson ?

: s₁.,l₁	d :-.r: m.f	s : m : s	l : ⌒—
Will ye	gang to Mains o'	Bungry, wi'	me ?

: l.dˡ	d :-.r: m.f	s : m : r.d	r.,m⁻: f
Will ye	gang to Mains o'	Bungry, Maggie	Anderson

: s	l : dˡ :-.l	s : m : r	d :—
My	bride and my	darling to	be ?

MAINS—Fine, man, fine! Noo, jist hear me,—(*sings*).

```
| s₁ .,l₁ | d  :- .r  : m.f | s  :  m  : r.d | r .,m  :  f⌢ |
| Will ye | gang to Mains o' | Bungry, Maggie | Anderson ?   |
```

```
: m .,m | r  : d | d  : t₁ | d  : d | —  ⫿
Will ye | gang  to Mains o' | Bungry ?
```

SOUTER—Stop, stop, min! Ye're intil French.—Listen again, and pey richt attention.

Sings first half of verse again, emphasising and keeping up the final note lah.

Noo, try that bittie first, and watch yersel'.

MAINS *sings as before, ending with an imitation of* SOUTER'S *final lah—*

```
                                           sf⟍⎯⎯⌢
: m .,m | r  : d | d  : t₁ | d  : d | — .s | ta  :— ⫿
Will  ye | gang to Mains o' | Bungry     wi' | me ? - -
```

SOUTER—(*laughing*) Na, na, Mains, that *winna* dee! Man, ye wid scare a caravan wife wi' howls like yon.—Try't alang wi' me.

They sing the verse together, MAINS *managing to keep the tune fairly well.*

MAINS—Man, Souter, ye'll jist need to come wi' me fin I gang to serenade Maggie. I could manage wi' you helpin' me.— Man, I say, come on wi' me to the Fair, and we can gae roon by Knowie's comin' hame.

Symphony is heard.

But hark! that's mair meesic.

Chorus (*heard without*)—

LADS AND LASSES TO THE FAIR.

Lads and lasses, to the Fair
Haste away, haste away;
Pleasure holds high revel there,
All the day, all the day.

See the sun so gaily gilding bank and brae;
Merry lark and lintie lilt along the way.

Hasten ere the golden hours of morn have run,
Hasten, lads and lasses, to the frolic and the fun.

> Lads and lasses, to the Fair
> Haste away, haste away;
> Pleasure holds high revel there,
> All the day, all the day.

SOUTER—(*rising and looking out*) It's a wheen young folks on their wye to the Fair. Fegs I canna resist the temptation. I maun come tee. (*Takes off apron and stands with* MAINS *listening till the music dies away*).
Come on till I get mysel' runkit, and I'll gae wi' ye. The fact is, I a kin' o' promised to look in at Knowie's mysel' the nicht. Ye see I'm some on for Maggie's sister, Jeannie.

MAINS—I see, I see. The vera thing, man. We'll be brithers : guid-brithers, ye ken.

SOUTER—(*taking* MAINS'S *arm*) Yes, companions-in-arms !

They march off whistling the refrain "Lads and Lasses."

[END OF SCENE II.]

———◇———

SCENE III.—KNOWHEAD.   EVENING.

JOHN ANDERSON *and his wife at fireside—the former reading newspaper, the latter darning.* MAGGIE *and* JEANNIE *at round table with cloth—sewing.*

JOHN ANDERSON—(*laying down newspaper*) Ye're unco quaet the nicht, you folk. Some o' you lassies micht gie's a bit sang to cheer's up a wee.

MAGGIE—Weel, fat'll't be, father ?

JEANNIE—Oh, I say, Maggie, gie's the "Bonnie Lass o' Fyvie."

JOHN A.—Ay, that's a fine-gaun ane. (*To wife*) Div'n ye think that, 'umman ? Ye min' ye eest to sing't yersel' lang syne ?

Mrs ANDERSON—Ay, it's a rale bonnie sang.

MAGGIE—(*sewing the while*) sings—

THE BONNIE LASS O' FYVIE.

There was a troop o' Irish dragoons
    Cam' marchin' up thro' Fyvie O,
And the Captain's fa'en in love wi' a very bonnie lass,
    And her name it was callèd pretty Peggy O.

O come down the stair, pretty Peggy, my dear,
    O come down the stair, pretty Peggy O;
O come down the stair, comb out your yellow hair,
    Take the last fareweel o' your daddy O.

It's braw, it's braw, a Captain's lady to be,
    It's braw being a Captain's lady O;
It's braw to rove and rant, and to follow with the camp,
    And to march when your Captain he is ready O.

The Colonel he cries, "Mount, boys, mount, boys, mount."
    "O tarry," says the Captain, "O tarry O.
O tarry, O tarry another day or two,
    Till we see if this bonnie maid will marry O.

"There's mony a bonnie lass into bonnie Auchterless,
    There's mony a bonnie lass in the Garioch O;
There's mony a bonnie lass into Fyvie's bonnie howe,
    But the brawest o' a' is pretty Peggy O."

It's when we cam' to Aul' Meldrum toon,
    We had our Captain to carry O;
And when we cam' to bonnie Aiberdeen,
    We had our Captain to bury O.

O bonnie grows the birk on bonnie Ythanside,
    And low lies the bonnie Lewes o' Fyvie O;
Our Captain's name was Ned, and he died for a maid,
    He died for the bonnie lass o' Fyvie O.

John A.—That's fine. There's naething like the auld sangs yet.

Knock heard.

Mrs A.—That's somebody chappin'. Rin, Maggie, lass, and see fa it is.

Maggie *goes to door, and returns with* Shepherd, *who carries parcel containing* Maggie's *boots.* Mrs Anderson *looks at him critically.*

John A.—Oh, it's you, Shepherd? Come awa' in by and gie's your crack. Ye'll hae been at the Fair?

Shepherd—(*taking chair which* Maggie *offers*) Ay, but I've been hame a while seen; and—and——happenin' to be at the Souter's, I thocht I micht—bring Maggie's boots wi' me.

Maggie—(*taking parcel from* Shepherd) O thank ye, Johnnie, thank ye.

Mrs A.—Thank him? Thank him for what I would like to ken.

Maggie—O mither!

Mrs A.—Yes, and Jeannie's had a fool's errand for the boots the day already. It was kindly meant, I've nae doot, young man, but quite unnecessar'—perfectly unnecessar'.

Maggie—But—mother——

Mrs A.—Never mind.—But isn't it time you lassies were gaun to your milkin'?

MAGGIE—But there's surely nae sic a hurry the nicht.

SHEPHERD—(*rising*) Oh, dinna lat me detain ye. I'm going at onyrate.

JOHN A.—Guidwife, ye're a kin' o' chasin' the young chap awa'.

Mrs A.—Oh, he needna go unless he likes, although it's aboot time a' dacent body was at their ain fire-en'.

SHEPHERD—Guid-nicht to ye a'.

JOHN A. and JEANNIE—Guid-nicht.

MAGGIE—(*hesitatingly, following* SHEPHERD *to door*) Guid-nicht, Johnnie.

SHEPHERD—Guid-nicht, Maggie.

Exit SHEPHERD

MAGGIE *returns with her apron at her eyes. She puts the boots away. She and* JEANNIE *get their milking pails and go out,* JEANNIE *patting her sister on the back.*

JOHN A.—Od, guidwife, ye wis hardly ceevil to the chap.

Mrs A.—Well, what's the use o' fellows like him comin' here?

JOHN A.—Young chaps will be young chaps, and ye canna help them comin' faur there's young lasses—Od, 'umman, ye min' fin I cam' coortin you ae Halloween nicht fin ye wis at Wastie's, ye min'?——

Mrs A.—Hold your tongue, John Anderson! Ye ken the chance oor Maggie has o' becomin' mistress o' Mains o' Bungry, and we canna hae her spoilin' her chance by encouragin' ony ither body.

JOHN A.—Weel, weel, you women folk see sae far afore ye; and maybe ye ken best.—But I think I'll awa' ben.

He rises, lights candle, and hobbles off with it and staff.
(*Looking round*) Ye'll min' and pit oot the cat. (*Exit*).

Mrs A.—(*alone*) Na, na, the chap's maybe guid and guid eneuch; but he's as peer's a kirk moose.

MAGGIE *and* JEANNIE *cross stage with pails.*

Ay, he's as peer's a kirk moose. And syne think what a chance Mains would be for Maggie. My certies! widna we haud up oor heids syne! (*Gets up and walks about affectedly*).

Re-enter MAGGIE *and* JEANNIE.

Noo, lassies, if your wark's a' deen I think it's aboot time ye were aff to your beds.

MAGGIE—I wid like to get this seam finished, and I think I will sit a while at the kitchie fire.

Mrs A.—Weel than; but dinna be sittin' owre late, min'.

Exeunt Mrs A. *and* JEANNIE. MAGGIE *resumes sewing.*

MAGGIE—(*alone*) O me! Anither case o' true love nae rinnin' smooth. (*Wipes her eyes*). Fat'll I dee? (*Stops and sighs. Resumes seam*). My mither, I can see, frowns on poor Johnnie. I ken fine she wants me to tak' Mains. . . . . . . Oh this wretched warldly spirit! . . . . But I'll be true to Johnnie— I will! Gin I dinna get him I'll never tak' nae ither body. . . never!

But hark! fat's that? I won'er gin a' the doors is steekit. This is the nicht o' the Fair. (*Goes to door and tries it*).

JOHNNIE *is heard without singing*—
"Mirk and rainy is the nicht."

It's Johnnie—jist Johnnie!—My!

She rises; moves about softly, putting things in order; goes to looking-glass on wall and touches up her hair, etc., smiling the while; and finally goes softly to door and opens it.

Enter SHEPHERD, *walking softly.*

SHEPHERD—(*in strong whisper*) Are they a' beddit, Maggie?
MAGGIE—Ay.
SHEPHERD—(*in natural voice*) Oh, that's fine. (*Sitting down and motioning* MAGGIE *to chair near him*) I'm awfu' gled I've seen ye again, Maggie.
MAGGIE—And I'm awfu' gled to see you, Johnnie.
SHEPHERD—(*moving his chair closer to hers*) Are ye, Maggie? Oh, that's fine. Ye ken I wis awfu' feart we wid be pairtet aifter fat happened the nicht.
MAGGIE—Pairtet we may be, Johnnie; but I can never like onybody sae weel's you.
SHEPHERD—(*moving his chair close to hers*) O Maggie, that's fine—it's awfu' fine!—Oh say't again!
MAGGIE—I can never like naebody sae weel's you Johnnie.
SHEPHERD—(*putting his arm about her and looking fondly in her face*) Ye dear lassie! . . . . But fat's yon? (*Moves his chair away in alarm*). There's somebody ootside.

MAINS *is heard at his serenade, blundering and beginning again, helped now and again by* SOUTER.

MAGGIE—(*rising to her feet in alarm*) It's some drunk fellows!

SHEPHERD *rises and looks about for means of escape.*

MAINS—(*without*) Ach! . . . Maggie!—Maggie An'erson! Hi! Maggie, I've come to see ye! Hi! open the door! Ye needna pretend ye're nae there. Hi! open the door or I'll bring doon the hoose!

He knocks loudly, and the SHEPHERD *in alarm gets under the table,* MAGGIE *adjusting the cloth to conceal him.*

Enter Mrs A., *somewhat in deshabille.*

Mrs A.—In a' the warld, Maggie, fat's adee?

MAGGIE—*(in agitation)* Some drunk men at the door!

MAINS—*(without, and again knocking)* Hi! Maggie, it's me; it's Mains!

Mrs A.—Dear me! It's Mr Sangster from Mains of Bungry!

Opens door. Enter MAINS.

MAINS—Oh! I beg your pardon, Mrs Anderson! I didna ken ye wis here. I—I——

Mrs A.—*(taking his hand)* Oh, never mind, Mr Sangster. Come awa' in-by. We're gled to see you at ony time, I'm sure.

MAGGIE—*(aside)* Ay, tho' it wis time a while ago for a' dacent body to be at their ain fire-en'.

Mrs A.—Maggie, get a chair for Mr Sangster.

MAGGIE *pushes forward chair ungraciously.*

MAINS—*(offering to shake hands)* Ay, Maggie lass, and are ye quite well, I thank ye?

MAGGIE—I'm fine, Mains.

MAINS—But jist failin' a wee bit in the hearin', eh?

MAGGIE *resumes sewing, and does not again look up.*

Enter JEANNIE.

And foo are ye, Jeannie lass?

JEANNIE—Oh, fine, Mains. . . . Are ye jist your lane?

MAINS—Yod, fin I mind on't noo, there's a chiel ootside wantin' to see you.

JEANNIE—Me?

MAINS—*(going to door and shouting)* Come awa in, Souter! Its a' richt! Come awa!

JEANNIE—Gracious me! The Souter! Fat wye's he here the nicht?

Enter SOUTER.

SOUTER—Good-evenin', freens.

Mrs A.—Good-evenin', Souter.

JEANNIE *sets chair for him against table.*

SOUTER—*(to* JEANNIE*)* Ye see I've come owre.

JEANNIE—Ay, and we're a' at hame, ye see; but ye're gey late.

SOUTER—We wis at the Fair, ye ken.

JEANNIE—Ye'll hae sweeties than.

SOUTER—Oh fairly. *(Producing bag of sweets)* There ye are, Jeannie lass.

JEANNIE—Oh, thank ye, Souter.

SOUTER—Ay, and Mains bocht a puckle tee—for Maggie, I'm jaloosin'.

MAINS—*(producing bag)* Ay, and here they are, Maggie lass.

MAGGIE—(*without looking up*) Oh, never min' me.   Ye can gie them to my mither.

Mrs A.—Maggie! (*To* MAINS) But I'll jist keep them for her,—(*aside*) till she's in a better humour.

(*To Souter*) And saw ye ony ferlies the day, Souter?

SOUTER—Oh ay, puckles.

JEANNIE—Ony lads and lasses, maybe?

SOUTER—Lads and lasses!—Mains and me wis the only chaps that cam' hame oor lanes.

MAGGIE—(*without looking up*) Good boys!

MAINS—(*to Souter*) Fa wis yon twa that turned aff oor road at Honeyneuk?—The chiel lookit like the Shepherd, didn' he?

SOUTER—Ay, I believe it hid jist been him—wi' Miss Fraser, nae doot.

MAGGIE—(*looking up*) It's a lee!

Mrs A.—Noo, Maggie, fat wye div ye ken? Yon's a fellow that I've jist *nae* faith in—jist a rale flee-b'-nichter.

MAINS—Ay, the Shepherd's an awfu' boy amo' the lasses, they say. He blaws aboot garrin' a' the women-folk rin aifter 'im, and him nae wantin' nane o' them.

SOUTER—Ay, but he'll tak' Miss Fraser, gin she'll only hae 'im.—The bawbees, ye ken.

MAGGIE—(*impetuously*) It's a' lees thegither!

SOUTER—Weel, weel, Maggie lass, we'll cheenge the subject. . . . . Fat thocht ye o' Mains's singin', b'wye?

MAGGIE—Singin'! Wis he singin'?

SOUTER—Ay, didn' ye hear 'im?

MAGGIE—I heard him roarin'; but I thocht it wis somebody hurtin' him.

SOUTER—Ha! ha! ha!—Mains man, that's intil ye! Ha, ha, ha!

He leans back with chair so as to tilt table a little.

MAINS—Noo, Souter man, that'll dee!

MAINS *pokes* SOUTER *in the breast, who loses his balance. Table is upset. General consternation,* MAGGIE *making vain attempt to conceal her lover.*

MAINS—(*in great excitement*) Murder! The Scoon'rel! Help! The Shepherd!

SHEPHERD *struggles to his feet.*

Haud him, Souter! Grip him! Lynch him, the villain!

JOHN ANDERSON *hobbles in.*

Help, Knowie! Your gun, Knowie! Sheet 'im!

MAINS *offers to seize* SHEPHERD.

SHEPHERD—Stand back, man, or I'll knock aff your heid!

MAINS—(*getting in behind* SOUTER) Souter man, tackle 'im! Ye're the fechtin' man, Souter. Intil 'im! I'll be needin' new Sunday beets afore lang.

> SHEPHERD *and* SOUTER *square at each other, moving about stage,* MAINS *keeping behind* SOUTER, *and* JOHN ANDERSON *always hobbling out of the way.* MAGGIE *hangs on* SHEPHERD'S *arm, and* JEANNIE *on* SOUTER'S.

Mrs A.—Noo, lat this disgracefu' scene end, and this vera minute, see! (*To* SHEPHERD) Hoo daur ye intrude in this wye intil a respectable hoose? (*To* MAGGIE) And, Maggie, I'm ashamed o' you—ashamed o' ye wumman, encouragin' the visits o' this low fellow!

SHEPHERD—Excuse me, Mrs Anderson, ye are a woman and Maggie's mother; but (*striking a fighting attitude*) daur ony man body to repeat what ye've said the noo, and by the Poo'ers—I'll brain 'im!

> SHEPHERD *stands a few moments. Then turns to door.*

MAINS—That's richt, man: ye've a bonnie back; and your absence is the best o' company!

SHEPHERD—(*turning at door*) Ay, but I'm nae deen wi' *you* yet; and, when we meet again, beware!

> *Exit* SHEPHERD.

MAINS—(*to* SOUTER) Fegs man! Awfu' business that! . . . But I'll surely succeed wi' Maggie noo. (*To* MAGGIE *who is moving away*) Maggie, lass, dinna gang awa'! Ye've lost a Shepherd, but ye've gained a Fairmer!

> *Exit* MAGGIE, *tossing her head.*

Mrs A.—Never mind, Mr Sangster, lassies are silly whiles, and need some management. . . . . . It'll a' come richt by-and-bye.

MAINS—Weel, weel, we'll hope sae at onyrate. . . . But I suppose there's nae eese bidin' ony langer the nicht. (*To* SOUTER *who is engaged with* JEANNIE) Are ye comin', Souter?

SOUTER—Na, I think I'll bide still a meenit. Oor roads, ye see, dinna lie the same wye noo.

MAINS—O ay, ye're wantin' to hae mair crack wi' Jeannie, ye rogue. It's a' richt. I'll jist need to be company to mysel'.— Guid-nicht to ye a'.

JOHN A., SOUTER, and JEANNIE—Guid-nicht, guid-nicht.

Mrs A.—(*accompanying* MAINS *to door*) Good night, Mr Sangster, and mind and haste ye back.

MAINS—Thank ye. I'll be rale gled to come back afore lang and see ye a'.—Guid-nicht.

> *Exit* MAINS.

Mrs A.—I'm some feart yon Shepherd fellow is aifter mischièf. He's maybe hingin' aboot to waylay Mains.

JOHN A.—D'ye think sae, guidwife? Then we'd maybe as weel see aboot that. You and me, Souter, could step alang the road a bit.

SOUTER—Vera good : I'm ready.

JEANNIE—Oh, ye're surely nae in sic an awfu' hurry?

SOUTER—Never mind, Jeanie lass, we'll be back again afore lang.

Mrs A.—(*anxiously to her husband who is preparing to set out*) Noo, I say, tak' care o' yersel', John Anderson; ye're gettin' some frail noo, ye ken.

JOHN A.—Ay, maybe I am; but (*striking floor with his stick*) I could gie a gey dunt yet, maybe.

Exeunt JOHN and SOUTER.

Mrs A.—Really, I'm growin' anxious aboot them a'. . . . This has been a maist unchancie nicht.

JEANNIE—Oh, jist a bit frolic. It'll be a' richt the morn aifter we sleep owre't.

Mrs A.—I only hope it may be; but d'ye ken I hae a strange presentiment o' something terrible gaun to happen, and I wish noo your father hidna gane oot.

Enter MAGGIE.

Knock at door.

O Maggie, gang to the door. I feel sae awfu' nervous.

MAGGIE *goes to door, and returns with PETER and POLICEMAN.*

Dear me, Peter! What in the warld's adee noo? Ye'll terrify me oot o' my judgment!

POLICEMAN—Don't be alarmed, Mrs Anderson; we're not after honest folk.—Has Mr Sangster of Mains of Bungry been here?

Mrs A.—Ay, Mains wis here, but he left a while ago.

POLICEMAN—Then we'll go after him. Was anybody with him?

Mrs A.—No; but my husband and anither man gaed aifter him.

POLICEMAN—Oh?

Mrs A.—Weel, ye see, there was jist a wee bit o' a disturbance at oor hoose the nicht—naething to signify, like; but yon shepherd chiel, John Murison, threatened Mains afore he left; and we were some feart Mains micht get a mischièf on the road hame.

POLICEMAN—I see. Well, Peter here reported to me that two suspicious characters were watching some of Mains's transactions at the Fair to-day, and I came along for fear he might be attacked by them on the way home. This is a new danger you mention, and between them Mains is in rather a bad way.—But we mustn't lose time. Come along, Peter, and let us follow up.

Peter—Ready! Guid-nicht, you folk.

Mrs A., Maggie, and Jeannie—*(faintly)* Guid-nicht.

Exeunt Policeman *and* Peter.

Mrs A.—O dear me! This is waur and waur! Something awfu' is *sure* to happen noo! . . . . May Heaven protect us and oors fae a' danger! . . . . Come, lassies!

Jeannie *sits at her mother's knee;* Maggie *stands by her side.*

Trio—Heavenly Power.

Heavenly Power, attend our cry,
  While lowly here we plead;
Be Thy gracious presence nigh
  In this lone hour of need;
Through the perils of the night
  Our loved ones safely guide,
And for ever in Thy light
  May they and we abide.

[End of Scene III.]

———◇———

SCENE IV.—HIGHWAY. BUSHES OR TREES AT SIDE. NIGHT.

Enter Shepherd, *singing*—

It's a' for want o' pocket-money,
  And a' for want o' cash,
Mony a bonnie laddie
  Maun leave his bonnie lass;
Love has been to me
  Like the dying o' a day;
A' for love o' you, lassie,
  I maunna stay.

(Speaks)—Ay, it's siller that rules the warld—siller that rules love and a'thing.—Naething but siller! Curse on it! *(Moving about excitedly)* O me! Fat'll I dee noo? . . . . Will I gang hame, or will I rin awa'? . . . . Will Maggie be true to me?—She said she wid. But oh, it's nae easy stickin' oot against her folk. And Mains wid be sic a bargain. *(Clenching his fist and shouting)* Mains—the auld villain!

John A. *and* Souter *appear at opposite side. They stop short and listen.*

I'll kill 'im! I will! I'll KILL 'im!

John A. *and* Souter *shake their heads to each other and retire.*

Shepherd *moves about, muttering to himself. Stops short.*

But hark! . . . . That's some folk comin' . . . I dinna

want to meet naebody the noo. (*Looks around*). I'll gang aff the
road till they gae by. (*Retires behind bushes*).

Enter Two Poachers.

1st Poacher—This is the road he must come, and this 'ere
spot will suit the job
 2nd Poacher—If we succeed, this should be a pretty good
night's work. Wasn't it Fifty-two Ten the dealer paid him?
 1st P.—That was the figure, mate.   The odd bit may have
gone in drams, but the Fifty will do—pretty tidy.
 2nd P.—Well, then, we know our game, don't we?   If he's
quiet, all right: if not—then. (*Producing pistol and pointing it
at imaginary victim*) I'll hold him up and you'll do the relieving
trick.
 1st P.—That's all right—Ha! ha! . . . .   But I think
we'll go along the road and see if he's coming.
 2nd P.—(*pocketing pistol*) Good!

Exeunt Poachers.

Shepherd—(*coming forward*) Ah! the villains!   I see their
game. They're to rob Mains, and maybe murder him—the bleed-
thirsty ruffians that they are! But I'll stop their game! By the
Poo'ers I will! Mains is my foe; but in the hour o' danger he'll
find I'm a man, and will defend my brither man to the death!
 . . . But hark! they're comin' back. (*Retires again*).

Enter Poachers.

1st P.—Be ready! Here he comes!

Mains *is heard coming along crooning his serenade.*
Enter Mains.

1st P.—(*to* Mains) Ay, it's a fine night, old chap.
 Mains—Oh, jist middlin'.
 2nd P.—(*stepping in front of* Mains *as he is passing on*) Stop,
guvnor, we want to know what o'clock it is.
 Mains—Eh?
 1st P.—What's the time, old chap?
 Mains—Weel, gin ye're awfu' anxious to ken, I wid say like
what we eest to dee at the skweel—It's half-past hangin' time,
steal fin ye like.
 1st P.—Thanks, old fellow; that's just what we mean to do.
So, just hand over your purse. We know what's in it. And your
watch, and any other trifle you may have about you.
 Mains—My purse and my watch? Man, ye're gyte!
 1st P.—Come along, sir—as quietly as possible, and at once.
It will save you trouble.
 Mains—(*shouting*) Never, man! Never!!
 2nd P.—(*producing pistol*) Hands up!
 Mains—Aff wi' yours! Murder! Help, hi! Thieves!

POACHERS *close on him.*

Murder! Help, hi! Murder!
SHEPHERD—(*rushing forward*) Villains! Clear out! Hi!!
(*Attacks* POACHERS).
MAINS—Hi! I'm doon! Help! Murder!!

SOUTER *rushes in.*

SOUTER—Mercy me! Fat's up here?
MAINS—Help! Help! They're robbin' me!

JOHN A. *hobbles in.*

JOHN A.—(*dunting with his stick*) Hi! Hi!

General melee, during which pistol goes off.

JOHN A.—O me! O me! I'm shot! Help, hi! I'm shot!
O me! (*Staggers and reels out of view*).

POLICEMAN *rushes in, followed by* PETER.

POLICEMAN—Hullo! What's up?

POACHERS *bolt, pursued by* SHEPHERD.

MAINS—(*lying on ground*) I'm robbit!
SOUTER—Ay, and Knowie's shot! (*Exit to attend to him*).
MAINS—Aifter the villains! Catch them! Hang them! I'm
robbit, and half killed! O me! O me!

Exit POLICEMAN *in pursuit.*

PETER—(*kneeling beside* MAINS) O Mains!
MAINS—Is that you, Peter? Aifter the villains, min! Catch
them! Hang them!
PETER—But fat aboot yersel', Mains?
MAINS—Never mind me! Aifter the scoon'rels, Peter!
PETER—Weel, weel. (*Rushes off*).
MAINS—(*alone*) O me! I'm robbit, and they say Knowie's
shot. . . . . Fat'll we dee? (*Gets to his feet with difficulty.
Limps about a little. Feels his leg*). Weel, gin that leg's nae
broken it's awfu' boo'd. But I'll maybe live lang eneuch to see
the villains hanged, and get back my siller. Jist think o't!
Fifty poun' odds, and the watch that I got fae my peer auld
granny fin I wis a loon. . . . Oh, I hope the bobby and
Peter 'ill catch them. . . . O me! But I maun see aboot
peer Knowie. (*Is limping off*).

Enter POLICEMAN *with* SHEPHERD *in charge, the latter
with traces of blood on face and hands.*

The Shepherd!
SHEPHERD—O Mains! Wisn' I helpin' you! And the bobby's

takin' me up. Wisn' 1 helpin' you, noo?

MAINS—Man alive! Fat wye div I ken? But I am robbit and Knowie's shot—That's fat *I* ken.

SHEPHERD—But I wis helpin' ye a' the time, min.

POLICEMAN—Why did you run then?

SHEPHERD—Man, I'm aye tellin' ye, I wis chasin' the robbers; and canna ye see for yersel that I've hid a struggle wi' them?

POLICEMAN—Well, that may be: we shall see; but you must come along with me meantime. (*To* MAINS) But how's old Anderson?

MAINS—I wis jist gaun awa' to see. The Souter's wi' 'im. (*Calling*) Souter! Come 'ere min!

Enter SOUTER.

Foo's peer Knowie?

SOUTER—He's sair hurtit, peer man. (*Seeing* SHEPHERD) Shepherd! You?

SHEPHERD—Ay, it's me, Souter. Canna *ye* say something for me?

SOUTER—Weel, ye're maybe jist as weel withoot *my* evidence.

POLICEMAN—Oh?

SOUTER—But I'm nae sayin' naething evnoo—min', I'm nae sayin' naething.

SHEPHERD—(*in despair*) O me! But this is a vile plot against an innocent man.—I'm innocent! I'm innocent!!

POLICEMAN—Well, as I have said, 1 hope you are; but you must come along with me just now. . . . We must see what like Anderson is.

MAINS—Ay, peer man; and get him hame. I'm some dwobble mysel', but gin we hid Peter back we sid maybe manage amon's. I doot the scoon'rels is clean awa'. O me!

Exeunt.

[END OF SCENE IV.]

———◇———

SCENE V.—ROOM IN POLICE STATION. LATE AT NIGHT.

SHEPHERD *lying on wooden dais asleep.*

Enter POLICEMAN, *carrying bunch of keys, followed by* MAGGIE, *with shawl about head.*

POLICEMAN—(*approaching dais*) Poor fellow, he's asleep. You can waken him yourself. . . . I'm sorry for him—sorry for you both.

MAGGIE—But he's innocent. They canna touch him. . . .
(*Appealingly*) They couldna touch a body that never did naething
—could they noo?

POLICEMAN—Ah—well—one must speak with caution. So much
depends on the evidence, you know. But we'll hope for the best.
Of course ·I must do my duty.

MAGGIE—Oh, I ken that. And it was very kind o' ye to lat
me in to see 'im the nicht, and it sae late.

POLICEMAN—Oh, that's all right. . . . But I'll leave you
now, and (*looking his watch*) I'll be back in a quarter of an hour.

MAGGIE—Oh, thank you, thank you : ye're very kind.

Exit POLICEMAN. MAGGIE *aproaches dais and looks
wistfully on* SHEPHERD. *Sings—*

> Sleep, my own, my loved one ;
> Angels guard thee now,
> Bless thy dreaming spirit,
> Crown with peace thy brow.—
>
> Hear my prayer, High Heaven,
> In this anguished hour,—
> In Thy mercy shield him,
> Save him by Thy power.

SHEPHERD—(*awaking, but dazed*) Maggie !—Fat is't ? (*Looking
round apartment*) Faur am I?

MAGGIE—O Johnnie !—Ye ken.

SHEPHERD—(*getting up and taking her hands*) O Maggie !
It wis awfu' good o' ye to come and see me.

MAGGIE—O Johnnie, this is terrible.

SHEPHERD—Ay, Maggie, it his been a terrible nicht this.
. . . . . And what aboot your father?

MAGGIE—The doctor his been, but he didna say much. I
think he's feart aboot 'im.—And what aboot yersel', Johnnie?

SHEPHERD—Weel, I dinna ken fat to think, Maggie. But ye
ken a' aboot it? And I am perfectly innocent, Maggie—ye
believe that?

MAGGIE—Yes, Johnnie, perfectly innocent. And what a shame
to tak' ye up !

SHEPHERD—Ah weel, maybe the Bobby couldna help makin'
a mistak'. I own I wis in an awfu' state fin he took me first ; but
the mair I think on't I aye grow the less feart. Fin a body his a
clear conscience they can face onything.

MAGGIE—That's true, Johnnie. But they canna touch ye.
They canna dee onything till a body that is innocent.

SHEPHERD—Ah weel, I'm nae jist sae sure o' that. The law's
gey queer sometimes, and a body never kens fat may happen.
Gin the truth comes oot I'm nae feart.

MAGGIE—But Providence will shield ye. It's aye on the side
o' the innocent.

SHEPHERD—Ay, we maun jist trust in Providence. It will bring a'thing oot richt in the lang-run, although we'll maybe suffer for a while.

MAGGIE—And fan will we see ane anither again, Johnnie?

SHEPHERD—Oh, I hope it winna be lang, Maggie; but—but, ye ken—I'm gaun to Aiberdeen the morn.

MAGGIE—O Johnnie!

SHEPHERD—But ye'll aye min' on's, Maggie?

MAGGIE—Ay, Johnnie—aye.

SHEPHERD—An'—An'—ye'll stick till's, Maggie?

MAGGIE—I'll aye stick to ye, Johnnie.

SHEPHERD—And ye winna—ye winna mairry Mains?

MAGGIE—Never, Johnnie, never! I'll never tak' 'im.

SHEPHERD—Oh that's fine, ye dear lassie! And ye'll be true to me, Maggie?

MAGGIE—Yes, Johnnie, true till death!

SHEPHERD—Oh ye darlin' lassie! Noo I can face onything!

MAGGIE—(anxiously) But the time's near up. The policeman wis to be back in a quarter o' an hoor; and we'll hae to say goodbye. I hope it winna be for lang, Johnnie.

Church clock without strikes midnight. They stand listening solemnly.

SHEPHERD—(awe-struck) Midnight, Maggie. . . . . Lat's say fareweel. . . . And may Heaven keep us baith till we meet again!

DUET.

Fare thee well, my own one;
Parting here in pain,
Knowing not if ever
We may meet again,—
Hear our vow, High Heaven,
Mark our plighted faith;
Changeless, unforgetting,
We are true till death.

Summertide and winter,
All the coming years,
Still thro' sun and shadow,
Still 'mid smiles and tears,
Love and faith undying
In this breast shall dwell,
Heart-enshrined for ever.—
Darling, fare thee well.

[END OF SCENE V.]

SCENE VI.—SCHOOLROOM.   AFTERNOON.

One or two forms and a desk. Blackboard, table and chair. Map on wall, etc. Ten or a dozen boys at lessons. General hum. DOMINIE at table, reading newspaper.
Boy (in kilts) comes up to DOMINIE with slate—a penny and a halfpenny on it. DOMINIE takes no notice of him for a while.

DOMINIE—(*looking up*) Well, John, have you got the right answer to that question now?

BOY—No, sir.

DOMINIE—Then what do you mean coming here? Didn't I tell you to work away till you got it right? Let me see how much you have done. . . . . (*Looks at slate*) Hullo! What's the penny and halfpenny here for?

BOY—Weel, than, I've been workin' at that question a' the aifterneen. I've gotten the answer a' but three bawbees, and I'll raither pey't mysel' than tchav ony langer wi't.

DOMINIE—(*shaking him up*) You young rascal! That's not arithmetic but impudence.

OLD WOMAN *bursts into Schoolroom.*

Did you knock, my good woman?

OLD WOMAN—Knock? No; but I'll seen dee't noo. I'll knock aff some o' that loons' heids!

DOMINIE—Well, if you put on better ones, I don't so much mind; but what's wrong with the boys?

O.W.—They're jist a wheen scamps, the hale lot o' them!

DOMINIE—Oh no; they're not quite so bad as that. Boys will be boys, you know.

O.W.—Ay, but they needna be run widifu's a'thegither.

DOMINIE—(*putting up his hand*) Hush, my good woman! That's too strong language for an old woman with one foot in the grave.

O.W.—Nane o' your haiverin' nonsense! My feet's baith in guid carpets that I bocht at Sandy Falconer's for auchteenpence.

DOMINIE, *carrying slate in left hand, turns head away, and unconsciously holds slate towards OLD WOMAN.*

Ye needna think ye'll gar me haud my tongue wi' a copper.

She gives the slate an unceremonious tilt, sending the coins spinning towards the boys, two of whom grab and pocket them, grinning at the owner who, still standing at the table, shakes an angry fist at the thieves.

DOMINIE—Come, come, this will do! What have the boys been doing to annoy you?

O.W.—Weel, than, the nickums steen't my deuks and broke ane o' their legs.

Dominie—Dear me! Was it a—a—fore leg?

O.W.—Ye auld sorra! Deuks hinna fore legs.

Dominie—Oh no; of course they have only two. How stupid of me! . . . . . Well that was very wrong of the boys.

O.W.—Ay, and some o' them pat a divot on the tap o' my lum, and near smor'd me wi' reek. (*Looking to a boy at end of seat*) And I'm sure it was you, Peter Pyper. (*Takes him by the ear, while boy cries out, and* Dominie *takes her by the arm, interjecting "Stop, stop!" once and again.*) Ye're a graceless scamp, min! I aye kent it, min! Ye're owre yer auld granny, min! Ye'll come to an ill en', min! An' ye'll be hangit afore ye dee, min! Ye scoon'rel, min!

Dominie—(*pulling her away*) Now, my good woman! You mustn't take law into your own hands, you know. I'll attend to discipline myself.

O.W.—Weel, gin ye dinna, I'll get the pleece to them. (*Shaking her fist at them as she goes out*) Ye set o' young blagairds!

Exit Old Woman.

Boy, *left at table, has moved to Blackboard, and with chalk drawn a picture of the* Old Woman *holding out her fist, writing below* THE WIFIE. *He now hastily rubs it out.*

Dominie *returns to him.*

Dominie—Go to your seat, sir.

Boy *sitting near has placed ink bottle on seat. The other, coming to his seat, sits down on bottle, and rises again with a yell.*

What's up? What's up?

Boy—(*blubbering*) Please sir, Tam Teuchit gart me sit doon on an ink bottle!

Dominie—Thomas Teuchit, stand up!

T. Teuchit—(*standing up*) Please, sir, I didna gar him. He sat doon himsel'.

Dominie—But you placed the bottle there?

T.T.—Weel, but he sid 'a lookit. The copybook says, Look afore ye sit doon.

Dominie—It says, Look before you leap. That is the proverb, sir.

T.T.—Weel, than, it's a' the same.—He loupit first and syne lookit.

Dominie—You are a young incorrigible, Thomas Teuchit. If you don't mend your ways you'll land in the Reformatory, or—somewhere else. You will bring me fifty lines written to-morrow. And boys, I am sorry to hear about you annoying the old woman. Let it never happen again, mind. (*Looking his watch*) But time's up. Put everything away. (*Bustle*). Now let us have a parting song; and then go home like good boys.—All stand!

Scholars join in some school song, and then march out.

DOMINIE—(*moving about and putting a thing or two in order*) Well, well, that's another day done. . . . One is so relieved when evening comes. . . . . But I must finish my paper. (*Walks up to chair and takes up newspaper.*) I've had so many interruptions in the course of the day that I haven't got it quite finished yet. Let me see: where was I? Oh yes: the next to the last column. (*Reads aloud to himself faked paragraph with humorous local allusion*).

Enter SHEPHERD *hurriedly, and in bit of plight.*

(*Throwing down paper and jumping up*) John Murison! You here? How in the world?——

SHEPHERD—(*interrupting*) O Mr Thomson, help me! He's aifter me! Hide me somewhere! (*Looks anxiously round School-room*).

DOMINIE—The policeman? You've escaped?

SHEPHERD—Ay, and he's comin'. I'm innocent! Help me! (*Moves about in restless alarm*).

DOMINIE—Yes, I'm convinced you are innocent, and I *will* help you if I can. Let me see: (*looking round*) there's no place here where you could be concealed. (*Thinking a moment*) Ah! I have it. There are some things of our dramatic club here. Wait a moment. (*Hurries to recess, and brings out long coat, old and worn, and old slouch hat*). On with these, quick! (SHEPHERD *puts them on while* DOMINIE *brings out long false beard, and fixes it on* SHEPHERD'S *face*). Now that's not so bad. But wait! (*Returns with lining pencil*). Now, hold up your face, and keep steady. (*Puts on wrinkles, etc. Standing back and looking at him*) Now your own mother wouldn't know you. One other thing and you are right. (*Brings a fiddle*). Now tune that, and you can be playing if the policeman comes in. (SHEPHERD *tunes fiddle, while* DOMINIE *looks off*). Yes, I declare, here he comes! Play up!

SHEPHERD *starts, say,* "Bonnie Lass o' Bon-accord."

Enter POLICEMAN *hurriedly.*

DOMINIE—(*to* SHEPHERD) Stop that horrid caterwauling, will you? People can't hear their own voice!

SHEPHERD—(*stopping, and in feigned voice*) Beg pardon, sir. No offence, sir. (*Saluting Policeman*) Good evenin', yer honour.

POLICEMAN — (*speaking hurriedly and breathlessly*) O Mr Thomson, excuse me, but have you seen John Murison, the Shepherd, pass this way just now?

DOMINIE—John Murison? Why, I understood you took him to Aberdeen this forenoon.

POLICEMAN—Well, I did set out with him this morning; but on the way to the station, you know, his dogs—they had got on our trail somehow—came up and went for me savagely. I was almost worried, and my prisoner escaped. To make a long story short, I started my man in Braeside Wood a little ago. He cut through the fields, and I lost sight of him just hereabout.

DOMINIE—Well, my scholars are not long out. Some of them may very likely have seen him. But really, after all, I can believe the poor fellow was innocent.

POLICEMAN—(*sharply*) I've got nothing to do with that.

DOMINIE—And if you want a job (*pointing to* SHEPHERD) here's the man you should take in charge—these dirty, gut-scraping, begging nuisances.

POLICEMAN—(*turning away impatiently*) Ach! Good-evening!

Exit POLICEMAN.

SHEPHERD—O thank ye, Mr Thomson, thank ye a thoosan' times! (*Taking* DOMINIE'S *hand*) And sae clever tee!

DOMINIE—Well, away you go! You should get well out of the country till the storm blows over, and your innocence be established, as I feel sure it will ultimately be.

SHEPHERD—But hoo am I ever to hear?

DOMINIE—Well, look here, my good fellow—you can make a pilgrimage back here in this same disguise; and, lest there should be any danger, you can use as a signal the tune you were playing just now.

SHEPHERD—(*hesitatingly*) And then there is—there is—Maggie —Maggie Anderson, ye ken.

DOMINIE—(*smiling*) Oh, yes, I know all about that. You want me to let Maggie into the secret? That's all right, trust me.— But you will need something to help you on the way. (*Taking out pocketbook*) Here's a five-pound note for you.

SHEPHERD—God bless you, Dominie! Ye'll get it back wi' interest some day, if I'm spared.

DOMINIE—That's all right, John. You were always a good honest lad. Nobody knows the folk in his district like an old dominie. I have faith in you; and that's why I have helped you. So off you go; and God bless you!

They shake hands in silence, both showing emotion.

Exit SHEPHERD.

DOMINIE *walks about.*

Well, well: a bit of a problem this in casuistry.—Should I have connived at John Murison's escape?—I am helping him to evade the law; but then law is only a means, justice being the

end. In John Murison's case the application of law would, I am
pretty certain, have eventuated in injustice—appearances being
so much against him. Being an innocent man he is entitled to
keep his liberty as an indefeasible right; and I, believing abso-
lutely in his claim to innocence, cannot refuse to help him when
he is only taking what belongs to him. . . . But what does
reasoning matter?—I am a man, and, sooner than help to send
John Murison to an undeserved jail, I'll go there myself!

Hurrahs heard without.

What's up now with our village youths and maidens?

Knocking heard. Dominie *goes to door.*

1st Youth—O Mr Thomson, hiv ye heard the news?—The
Shepherd his escapit!

Dominie—Has he? And you're all rejoicing over the event?

1st Youth—Oh, fairly! We're a' delighted. Aren't ye, Mr
Thomson?

Dominie—Well, I can't say I'm particularly sorry, believing
as I do that John Murison is quite innocent; and if your merry
band cares to come into the schoolroom, I shall at least be pleased
to see how you can rejoice.

1st Youth—(*calling to companions without*) Come on, lads
and lasses! Come on, ane and a'!

Youths and Maidens file into schoolroom.

1st Youth—Three cheers for the Shepherd!

Company cheer.

2nd Youth—(*to* Dominie) Oh, I say, Mr Thomson, couldna
we hae a dance on the heids o't, fin we're a' here?

Dominie—Well, I have no objection, say, to a reel; but where
will you get the music?

2nd Youth—I hiv't!—We met an auld fiddlin' mannie jist
ootside there: we'll catch him and fess him back.

Dominie—Oh yes, that's the old fellow that was in here a little
ago. He can play; but I don't know if he'll be willing to come
back.

2nd Youth—Nae fear o' that; we'll gar 'im.

1st Youth—Ay, and gin he winna come on's ain feet we'll
cairry 'im.—(*To* 1st Youth) Come on, Jeck, you and me!

Exeunt Two Youths.

Dominie—(*to Company*) Well, I suppose we may take it for
granted that our two heroes will capture the old fiddler; and, to
save time, you might be arranging yourselves. (*Putting his hand
on a youth's shoulder*) Come, Willie, you'll be floormaster. Get
them into their places, and mind to leave room for our two free-
booters when they return.

Youth *arranges Company for reel.* Enter Two Youths,
with Shepherd *in charge.*

1st Youth—Here's oor man!

2nd Youth—Ay, and he'll fairly play, noo that we've nailt
'im.

Dominie—*(to* Shepherd) So you're here again, Mr Fiddler?
You see it is easier escaping from foes than friends.

Shepherd—*(always in feigned voice)* That's so, sir.

Dominie—Well, your captors have no doubt told you what
you are wanted for. Are you willing to oblige them by playing
a Reel?

Shepherd—Delighted, sir.

Shepherd *takes seat. Tunes fiddle, plays Reel.*
Company dance.

Dominie—That's good.

1st Youth—Ay, it's capital; but we'll need to remember the
fiddler noo.   Come, you folk, fin your pouches.   (*Goes round
Company with bonnet collecting coppers. Presents collection to*
Shepherd).   Here, my man.   Ye've deen famous; and we're
awfu' muckle obleeged till ye.

Shepherd—*(accepting collection)* Thank you, sir; thank you,
ladies and gentlemen, one and all.

Dominie—Now, Mr Fiddler, you have played a spring for our
departed friend; couldn't you now sing a farewell stave for him,
as a wind-up to our happy meeting?

Shepherd—Delighted, if I could, sir. I used to sing, but my
voice is a bit gone now.

Dominie—No fear of that. It's not so very long ago since I
heard you singing like a Trojan.

Shepherd—Well, just to oblige you all, we'll try. (*Reflecting*)
Let me see.—"Guid-nicht and joy be wi' ye a',"—would that do?

Dominie—The very thing for the occasion. Quite a happy
idea.

Shepherd—And you'll all join in the chorus?

Company—Surely, surely.

Shepherd *advances to centre of Company. Sings, Company*
joining in Chorus.—

GUID-NICHT AND JOY BE WI' YE A'.

The evening sun's gaen doon the west,
    The birds sit noddin' on the tree;
All nature now prepares for rest,
    But rest prepared there's nane for me.

Cho.—Guid-nicht and joy, guid-nicht and joy,
 Guid-nicht and joy be wi' ye a';
For since it's so that I must go,
 Guid-nicht and joy be wi' ye a'.

I grieve to leave my comrades dear,
 I mourn to leave my native shore,
To leave my aged parents here,
 And the bonnie lass whom I adore.

Cho.—Guid-nicht and joy, &c.

But tender thoughts maun now be hushed,
 When danger calls I must obey;
The transport waits us on the coast,
 And the morn I will be far away.

Cho.—Guid-nicht and joy, etc.

[END OF ACT I.]

ACT II.

SCENE I.—ROOM IN LAIRD'S MANSION.

MORNING.

LAIRD, *in dressing gown, sitting in easy chair and smoking cigar.*
Sings—

It's oh for the good old days,
 Of castle, keep, and moat,
When the King was King, and the Laird was Laird,
 And all besides was nought.

Then we made all the laws ourselves,
 Which was the proper way;
Now every cur of a commoner
 Must have his vote and say.
  Then it's oh for the good old days, &c.

Then each man for to please the Laird
 Would be hanged with a pleasant grace;
Now a crofter dares show insolent airs,
 And grumbles to your face
  Then it's oh for the good old days, &c.

Each man would claim his bit
 Of heather, whin, and broom,
Get a court to fix his rent, and sit
 Secure till the day of doom.
  Then it's oh for the good old days, &c.

They're to go for the House of Lords,
Give women-folk a vote;
Till the British Con—sti—tu—ti—on
Goes simply all to pot.

Then it's oh for the good old days,
Of castle, keep, and moat,
When the King was King, and the **Laird** was **Laird,**
And all besides was nought.

Knock.

LAIRD—Come in.

Enter PAGE.

Well, Charles?

PAGE—Two gentlemen wish to see you, sir.
LAIRD—Who are they?
PAGE—Tenants, sir, I think, sir.
LAIRD—Oh, you can just show them up.
PAGE—Yes sir.   (*Exit*).
LAIRD—(*alone*) No doubt wanting something or other—**reduc**tion of rent, drain pipes, or something. Beastly nuisance, **you** know! But I'll just hand them over to my factor.

Knock.

LAIRD—Come in!
Enter PAGE, *introducing* MAINS *and* SOUTER.
PAGE—Mr Sangster and Mr Birse, sir.
LAIRD—Oh, come away, gentlemen! So pleased to **see you.** Pray be seated.

Exit PAGE.

MAINS *and* SOUTER *take chairs, latter keeping on his cap.*
MAINS—(*nudging his companion*) Souter, min, tak' aff **your** bonnet, min!
SOUTER—Oh, I beg pardon! (*Snatches off cap and sits on it*).
LAIRD—Well, friends?
MAINS—Weel, ye see, we've jist called on you aboot a bit o' business, Sir Jeems.—The Souter here,—he's nae an ill breet ava', the Souter, ye ken—
SOUTER—Mains, min!
MAINS—And he his plenty o' gab fin he's sittin' in's ain bit choppie, cain' tackets intil an auld beet, but——
SOUTER—Mains, min; oh, I say, min!
MAINS—(*paying no attention*) But fin he comes afore his betters he's jist some blate, ye ken; and sae I cam' owre the gate wi' 'im the day.

LAIRD—That was very kind of you, Mr Sangster: and what particular errand was your friend on?

MAINS—Oh, weel, ye see, Laird, the Souter here's thinkin' o' gettin' mairriet——

SOUTER—Mains, *Mains*, min! Fat are ye at, min? Weesht, min!

LAIRD—(*smiling*) Oh, it's all right. That's nothing to be ashamed of. Quite the reverse, I assure you, quite the reverse. Well, Mr Sangster, pray proceed.

MAINS—Weel, as I wis sayin', the Souter's gaun to get mairriet. Noo, there's that place o' Waulkie's that will be oot at Whitsunday. The Souter's maybe nae great fairmer as yet, haein' hid mair to dee wi' batter-horns than short-horns, and kennin' mair aboot rossetty-ends than end-rigs; but the lass he's gettin'—she's a dother o' auld Knowie's, ye ken——

SOUTER—*Mains*, min! I say, min! Stop min!

MAINS—(*turning on Souter*) Noo, Souter, is't you or me that's to mak' this speech? Afore I proceed ony forder, is't you or me?—Answer me that!

LAIRD—(*laughing*) Yes, I think, shoemaker, you may as well let your friend proceed in his own way. We all understand the situation quite well.

MAINS—Weel, as I wis sayin' when the Souter interrupit me, the lass he's gettin' his a thorough acquantance wi' country affairs and beasts' mait.——

Knock.

LAIRD—Come in.   (*Enter* PAGE).   Well, what is it now, Charles?

PAGE—Please, sir, the gamekeeper wants to see you, sir.

LAIRD—Tell him I'm engaged just now, but will see him presently.

PAGE—But please, sir, he says his business is urgent. They have caught two poachers, sir.

LAIRD—Oh, that's it, is it? Well, just send them up.

PAGE—Yes, sir.   (*Exit*).

LAIRD—We can just interrupt our discussion for a little till I see those fellows and give orders about them.

Enter GAMEKEEPER *with* TWO POACHERS.

SOUTER, *recognising them, rises hurriedly.*

SOUTER—Will ye excuse me a minute, Sir Jeems?

LAIRD—Oh, certainly, Mr Birse.

Exit SOUTER.

(*To* GAMEKEEPER) Well, John, whom have you got here?

G. KEEPER—Please, sir, these are two fellows we caught poaching in the Braeside Wood.

Laird—Oh, indeed; and had they anything in their possession?

G. Keeper—Yes, sir; they had a couple of hares, some half-dozen rabbits, and nets.

Laird—This is serious. (*To* Poachers) Now, what have you got to say for yourselves?

1st Poacher—May it please your Honour, it is the first time we've been at this. We were out of work and were driven to it by want; but, your Honour, if you let's off we'll never do't again, your Honour.

2nd Poacher—No, your Honour, we'll never, never do't again.

G. Keeper—Great liars and scoundrels! We've been watching you for a week, and we were on your track before, about six months ago.

Laird—Ah! we must look into this.

Enter Souter *hurriedly.*

Souter—Noo, Laird, wid ye alloo me to say a word aboot thae chaps?

Laird—Certainly, shoemaker, we shall be very pleased indeed to have any information you can give.

Souter—(*in great excitement*) Weel!—Weel!—Weel!——

Mains—Weel *what*, ye gowk?

Souter—Weel, than,—that's the twa that robbit Mains, and shot Knowie.

Mains—(*springing to his feet*) Great Scott!

Poachers *make a bolt for the door.*
Policeman *confronts them in door.*

Policeman—Halt! (Poachers *stop short*).　Surrender!　In the King's name I arrest you both!

Poachers *yield and are handcuffed.*

Laird—Bravo, Constable! and well done, Shoemaker!

Mains—(*waving his bonnet*) Ay, hip, hip, hurray!
(*To* -Poachers) Ay, lads, wid ye like to ken fat o'clock it is noo? (*Taking out his watch and looking at it*) It's jist aboot five-and-twenty minutes to Peterheid.　So ye'll better hurry up!

Laird—Yes, and we'll give them a convoy to the door.—Lead on, Constable.

Exeunt.

[End of Scene I.]

SCENE II.—KNOWEHEAD.   EVENING.

MAGGIE *sitting at fireside, sewing.*

Sings—

Aye waukin' O,
Waukin' aye and weary!
Sleep I can get nane
For thinkin' on my dearie.

Spring's a pleasant time,
Flowers o' every colour;
The birdies build their nests,
And I think on my lover.

When I sleep I dream,
When I wauk I'm weary;
Sleep I can get nane
For thinkin' on my dearie.

Knock.

Enter DOMINIE.

DOMINIE—Good evening, Maggie.

MAGGIE—(*rising and taking* DOMINIE'S *hand*) Oh, good evening, Mr Thomson.

DOMINIE—(*taking a chair*) I came over to tell you the news of the court, which I have just heard.

MAGGIE—That was very kind. And how has the trial gone?— Oh, tell me!

DOMINIE—Well, the men have been convicted, and sentenced to seven years' penal servitude.

MAGGIE—Thank Heaven for that!

DOMINIE—Yes; and the men themselves have cleared John Murison of all complicity in the crime; nay, have confirmed what John himself claimed, and what we have all along firmly believed, that he attacked them in defence of Mains.

MAGGIE—Oh, what a relief!—And noo Johnnie can come back?

DOMINIE—Yes, Maggie—but——

MAGGIE—But what?

DOMINIE—Well, I am very sorry indeed, my dear girl, to speak of a cloud when your sky seems otherwise so bright.

MAGGIE—Oh, what is it? Tell me!

DOMINIE—Well, I have learned—from a correspondent—that our friend joined the army after leaving this.

MAGGIE—Oh!

DOMINIE—And his regiment has been abroad, and has suffered rather heavily in a recent battle.

MAGGIE—Oh!

Dominie—Now, Maggie, do not place undue stress on this.
—There may be some confusion of names; and, in fact, I think
it not at all improbable that John Murison changed his when he
joined the army.

Maggie—Oh, but ye dinna say there's bad news aboot *him*?

Dominie—Not necessarily about *him*, mark you. As I said,
we cannot be at all sure about the name applying.

Maggie—But oh, what *has* happened? Tell me! This sus-
pense is dreadful! Is he—is he—oh, is he killed? Oh!! (*Buries
her face in her hands*).

Dominie—(*laying hand on her shoulder*) Now, do be calm,
my dear girl. I sympathise with you very deeply, even in your
apprehensions. But do not let these overwhelm you. Do not take
too gloomy a view of the situation. There *is* a John Murison in
the list of those who have fallen; but we can't be sure it is our
friend. Let us hope meantime it is not.

Maggie—(*sobbing, then rising agonised*) O Johnnie! Johnnie!!
(*Covers her face with her hands and goes out*).

Dominie—Poor girl! Poor girl! (*Moves about, wringing his
hands*).

Enter Mrs Anderson *hastily.*

Mrs A.—Dear me, Mr Thomson, what's ado?

Dominie—(*shaking hands*) I am sorry, Mrs Anderson, I've had
to be the unwilling bearer of bad news to poor Maggie—un-
confirmed, however, it is some relief to add.

Mrs A.—Oh me! What has happened?

Dominie—John Murison, the shepherd, you know—it is so very
sad—to stand acquitted to-day, and——

Mrs A.—Well, what about him?

Dominie—He enlisted on leaving this, and there is some
reason to fear he has fallen in battle.

Mrs A.—Oh, that's sad. I'm sorry to hear that.

Dominie—And poor Maggie—if it should prove true.

Mrs A.—She'll nae doot feel't some at first, but I'm hopefu'
she'll get owre the thing by-and-by.

Dominie—Mrs Anderson!

Mrs A.—Oh weel, ye see, Mr Thomson, we never jist a'
thegither approved o' that attachment o' Maggie's, ye ken.

Dominie—(*severely*) Oh yes, I understand; but it's very tragic
all the same. . . . But I must be going. . . . Good evening,
Mrs Anderson.

Mrs A.—(*shaking hands*) Good evenin', Mr Thomson.

Exit Dominie.

Ah! noo the wye is clear! I'm sorry for the lad; but, ye see,
it's jist the deein's o' Providence, and we maun bow to His will.
. . . . And jist to think o't happenin' at this crisis, when we

are on the very verge o' destitution! Fegs, a body wid think Providence had speecially interposed. . . It's jist *wonderfu'*.

Enter JEANNIE, *dressed.*

Weel, Jeannie, ye've gotten back?—And hoo hiv they gotten on wi' the factor?

JEANNIE—Oh, it's a' richt, as Mains wid say. They've ta'en the place.

Mrs A.—And what's to be the rent?

JEANNIE—The factor wis seekin' seventy-five pounds, the greedy rascal; but Mains gart him tak' seventy.

Mrs A.—That's fine. *Ye'll* be richt at onyrate, Jeannie, gin we only hid peer Maggie as weel sattled.—Wid ye send her ben?

JEANNIE—Surely. (*Exit, singing a cheerful snatch*).

Enter MAGGIE, *tearful and sad.*

Mrs A.—Noo, Maggie dear, jist sit doon till we speak it owre. . . . . I'm awfu' sorry to hear the sad news that the Dominie has brocht.

MAGGIE—But, mither, he's nae sure if it be true. It's maybe nae him.

Mrs A.—Ah, lassie, dinna big your hopes on that. Ill news is aye owre true.—Noo, Maggie, I think ye ken my wishes in the maitter.

MAGGIE—Oh ay, I ken them fine; but it canna be; there's nae eese o' sayin' onything mair aboot that.

Mrs A.—Noo, Maggie, listen to me. Ye ken we hinna been very weel aff sin' your peer father wore awa'. But ye dinna ken the warst—na, ye dinna ken the warst.

MAGGIE—Oh!

Mrs A.—Ay; and it's come to this, that, unless we get help, we'll hae to leave the place. Jist think o't—haein' to leave the auld place—to leave Knoweheid faur I've spent the best and happiest days o' my life! (*Using handkerchief*) O dear! O dear!

MAGGIE—Mother, mother!

Mrs A.—(*tearfully*) Yes, Maggie; *you* are young and strong yersel', and can easy tak' a place; but there's naething for your peer auld mither but the Peershoose. (*Handkerchief again*). Weel, weel!

MAGGIE—Mother, mother! Ye ken I wid dee onything to save you fae that.

Mrs A.—Weel, ye ken, Maggie, there's but ae wye—only *ae* thing can help us; and I leave you to think it owre, and mak' up your mind aboot it. (*Rises and leaves room*).

MAGGIE—(*calling after her*) Mother! mother!—(*Alone*) Oh, what can I dee? . . . . What *can* I dee? Even if Johnnie never comes back, I canna mairry anither. I can never tak'

Mains! . . . But then to think o' my peer auld mither, wi' her high notions, haein' to leave the auld hame and face poverty amo' frem't folk! . . . And she pits't on me to save her by takin' Mains. . . . O me! What *will* I dee?

Knock. Enter MAINS, *softly and slowly.*

MAINS—(*kindly*) Maggie lass, I've heard it a', and ye hae my deepest sympathy. (*Shaking hands*).

MAGGIE—Thank ye, Mains. (*Looks on floor*).

MAINS—(*after a pause, tenderly but hesitatingly*) And, Maggie, will it mak' ony difference—ony difference, that is to say, in oor relations to ane anither? . . . Hae I ony better a chance, that's to say, noo that Johnnie's awa', peer stock?

MAGGIE—But oh, Johnnie's maybe livin', and will return yet.

MAINS—But if he *never* comes back?

MAGGIE—I can never love anither.

MAINS—But ye micht *like* anither, maybe, ye ken.

MAGGIE—Like's nae love.

MAINS—No! the same's a calf's nae a coo; but gin ye wyte, the calf grows a coo; and sae, beginnin' wi *like*, ye'll maybe come to *love* by-and-by.

MAGGIE—Never! Atween like and love there's a gulf that canna be crossed.

MAINS—Weel, lattin' ye aff wi' that; suppose a body wis to be content wi' like, fat wid ye say to *that*, Maggie?

MAGGIE—O Mains!

MAINS—(*more eagerly*) And ye maybe ken foo muckle it wid mean to your mither and ye a'?

MAGGIE—Yes, I ken that—I ken a' that.

MAINS—Winna ye think on't than, Maggie? Winna ye dee't for your peer auld mither's sake? It's *you* that can keep a reef abeen her heid, and mak' her widowed years comfortable and happy. And will ye say na, and see her turned oot to the cauld warld, hooseless and penniless? . . . . Can ye dee't? . . .

MAGGIE *hides her face.*

I say, Maggie An'erson, *can ye dee't?*

MAGGIE—O Mains, hae pity on me! Ye'll brak my hert!

MAINS—Forgie me, Maggie; but oh, say, is there ony hope? Tell me, Maggie, is there *ony* hope ava?

MAGGIE—O Mains, what can I say? I'm in an awfu' strait. But ye ken I wid dee onything for my mither's sake—onything that my conscience will lat me dee. (*Rises, and moves away*).

MAINS—(*to* MAGGIE *as she goes out*) Then there *is* hope? (*Exit* MAGGIE). Yes, there is—there is! I ken! I'm sure! (*Getting to his feet and looking about*) Man alive! Faur am I? . . . That blink o' love and hope his surely turned my heid! (*Indulges in demonstrations of joy*). Fegs, I'm surely gyte! . . Nae feel like an auld ane!

Enter Mrs A., *beaming.*

Oh, come awa', Maggie, my darlin'! (*Takes hold of her and swings her round as in a reel*).

Mrs A.—Mr Sangster!

MAINS—Oh, I beg your pardon, Mag—Mrs—Mrs John Anderson, my jo! . . . Fegs, I *am* gyte!

Mrs A.—Yes, I see that, Mr Sangster; and I'll jist sit doon till ye come to yersel'. (*Sits down*).

MAINS—(*also sitting down*). Weel, that's some steam aff. . . (*Mops his face with big red handkerchief*). Fegs, I ken it's nae richt to gang on in this gate, espeecially on the heids o' a peer chap's death; but I couldna help mysel'—I jist couldna help mysel'.—But I'll tell ye fat I'll dee. I'll put up a stane in the kirkyaird to John Meerison; and it'll be a guid ane tee, min'; for the Shepherd wis a guid honest chiel, and dee'd at last in defence o' his country. . . . Will that dee, Mrs Anderson?

Mrs A.—Ay, Mains, it's awfu' good o' ye to min' on sic a thing; and folk will think a' the mair o' ye for't.

MAINS—Weel, *that's* a' richt.—(*Eagerly*) But fat aboot Maggie? Did she tell ye a' aboot it—fan it's to be, and a' the lave o't? Did she pit ye throw't a'?

Mrs A.—Weel, she his admitted sae muckle; but we maun gie her time. Ye see she aye clings to the hope that John Murison may be alive yet.

MAINS—Him alive! I'll warrant he's as deid's a door nail.— Didn' I tell ye that a stane was gaun up till 'im in the kirkyaird?

Mrs A.—A' the same, we canna force her into oor wye o' lookin' at the thing. We'll need to hae patience, and wyte till she sees't for hersel'.

MAINS—Wyte? I'll wyte a hun'er thoosan' years for Maggie Anderson!

Mrs A.—(*smiling*) Less than that will dee.

MAINS—Weel than,—sax months?

Mrs A.—Maybe.

MAINS—The back o' hairst?

Mrs A.—Ay, that micht dee. A' diffeeculties should be oot o' the road by that time.

MAINS—Weel, than, that's a' richt than.—The back o' hairst. —That's a' richt than? (*Rising*) But I maun awa' hame and begin this vera nicht to mak' things ready at Mains o' Bungry.— Ye see sax months will seen gae by. (*Takes Mrs A.'s hand, and keeps shaking it warmly*) Good-bye, than, Mrs Anderson. Goo—ood-bye! (*Patting her on shoulder*) Ye're an *awfu'* fine wifie; and I *div* like ye!

Mrs A.—(*simpering*) O Mr Sangster!

Exit MAINS, *singing*—

Now's the day, and now's the hour,
See the front of battle lour,
See approach proud Mains's power,—
     Mains o' Bungeree!

Mrs A. *stands at door looking after him*
Comes forward.

Fine man Mains; and awfu' likable.—I never kent he wis sic a fine man.

Weel, but this is maybe a gey business noo, and a body hardly kens fat to think aboot it.—Fegs, Maggie's maybe richt aifter a'. I could weel believe the Shepherd's *nae* deid. He'll likely eneuch be back for Maggie. Ay, and even suppose he disna come back the noo, it widna jist be vera safe for Maggie to tak' Mains. He micht come back aifterhin; and syne it wid be "Auld Robin Gray" owre again. Na, it widna jist be vera safe.

Of coorse it wid be an awfu' pity for Maggie to loss sic a fine doon-sit as Mains o' Bungry wid be; and Mains himsel' sic a fine man. Ay, it *wid* be a pity to loss him oot o' the faimly. But (*stepping up to looking-glass on wall and surveying herself*) ye're nae jist sic an auld-like woman yersel', Mrs Anderson. Na ! And, (*posing*) tho' I say't mysel', there's waur lookin' folk maybe. Queer things, ye ken, fyles turns roon in this warld. There's nae jist sayin' *fat* micht maybe happen. (*Moving off*) Na, there's nae sayin'.—And Mains is sic a fine man, ye ken. (*Exit*).

[END OF SCENE II.]

———◇———

SCENE III.—HARVEST FIELD, WITH A FEW STOOKS. MID-DAY.

Harvesters resting after meal which HOUSEKEEPER *and Servant have carried to field—in various positions, reclining against stooks, etc.—*PETER *seated on top of ale-barrel. Scythes and Rake.* HOUSEKEEPER *and Servant collecting dishes in big Basket.*

PETER—Weel, fa says for a sang noo?

HARVESTER—A good move, Peter. (*To Girl*) Annie, ye'll gie's "Johnnie Sangster."

PETER—Ay, and we'll a' pit in a chorus. Ilka body maun join in; min' that noo. (*Advances to stook nearest front, and lies down out of sight of rest. Secretly motions to* HOUSEKEEPER, *who has finished her task. She comes with basket, and sits down beside him*).

HARVESTER—Noo, gin ye're a' sattled, Annie's ready to begin.

Girl sings—

JOHNNIE SANGSTER.

O' a' the seasons o' the year,
   When we maun work the sairest,
The harvest is the foremost time,
   And yet it is the rarest.
We rise as seen as mornin' licht,
   Nae craters can be blither;
We buckle on oor finger-steels,
   And follow oot the scyther.

Cho.—For you, Johnnie, you, Johnnie,
   You, Johnnie Sangster,
   I'll trim the gavel o' my sheff,
   For ye're the gallant bandster.

A mornin' piece to line oor cheek,
   Afore that we gae forder,
Wi' cloods o' blue tobacco reek
   We then set oot in order.
The shaves are risin' fest and thick,
   And Johnnie he maun bind them;
The busy group, for fear they stick,
   Can scarcely look behind them.

For you, Johnnie, etc.

If e'er it chance to be my lot
   To get a gallant bandster,
I'll gar him wear a gentle coat,
   And bring him gowd in handfu's;
But Johnnie he can please himsel',
   I widna wish him blinkit;
Sae, aifter he has brewed his ale,
   He can sit doon and drink it.

For you, Johnnie, etc.

[*During the singing of the verses,* PETER *from time to time exchanges glances with his companion. During the chorus he whispers to her, and indulges in endearments, only joining in last word "bandster," which he delivers lustily, prolonging the last syllable beyond everybody else*].

Enter MAINS.

MAINS—Weel, you folk; and ye're jist haein' a bit sang to keep up your speerits and haud doon your denner, I suppose. (*Looking round*) But faur's Peter? (PETER, *who has hold of* HOUSEKEEPER'S *hand, relinquishes it, and edges away*).

HARVESTER—(*pointing*) He's at the back o' yon stook, coortin' wi' the hoosekeeper. (*Harvesters laugh*).

MAINS—Is he, the rascal?

PETER—Fat's that ye're sayin', Geordie Dempster? (*Has got on his knees, taken out a few plates, and is busily packing them again*). I'm helpin' Jessie here to pack the dishes richt. (*To* MAINS, *who has come forward*) See for yersel', Mains.

MAINS—Ay, he's at that job—the noo.

PETER—(*rising to his feet*) That sid be aboot richt noo, Jessie.

HOUSEKEEPER—Thank ye, Peter; ye're awfu' handy.

HARVESTER *laughs*.

PETER—O man, Geordie, ye think yersel' awfu' clever! A body wid easy ken fa teem'd the bowie.

MAINS—Weel than, Peter, if ye're quits wi' Geordie, fan micht ye be throw wi' the cuttin', think ye?

PETER—Oh, I think we sid hae clyack some time the morn.

MAINS—That's good. Weel, we've hid splendid weather, and I'm sure it's to continue. And man, we hae a grand crap a' owre. I dinna think I ever saw the like o't on Mains o' Bungry.

PETER—Ay, I'll warrant there's aucht quarters to the ackre a' owre.

MAINS—Ay, there's a' that. And corn's an extra price the year, and aye like to rise. We'll be in nae hurry thrashin' oot.—Na.

Two shots heard without.

Hillo!

Dead bird falls among stooks. He picks it up.

Ay, but ye're a gratefu' beastie, maybe. Ye come back to the folk that fed ye. Hae, Peter (*offering him bird*). This'll be a tasty denner to your auld mither.

PETER—(*stuffing it under his smock*) Thank ye, Mains.

MAINS—(*moving about and putting down heads of stooks*) The Laird'll likely be in aboot.

Enter GAMEKEEPER, *carrying gun and bag.*

Ay, ay, Gamie, and ye're jist haein' a bit shot?

GAMEKEEPER—Just that, Mains.

MAINS—And is the Laird wi' ye?

G.-KEEPER—Yes, he's coming up the other side of the field. I'll have to wait for him. (*He turns to* PETER, *while* MAINS *looks off for* LAIRD. *Then he gets into conversation with* HOUSEKEEPER, *while* PETER *hangs around, darting angry glances at the pair*).

Shot heard without.

PETER—(*approaching and lifting basket as if to feel its weight*) This is gey heavy, Jessie. I can gie ye a lift owre the dyke wi't.

H.-KEEPER—Oh, I'm in nae hurry, Peter.

PETER—Ye'll as weel tak' a body fin ye can get them. We'll be startin' again in a fyow meenits. (*Proceeds a step or two. Stops and looks round.* HOUSEKEEPER *seems to follow reluctantly*). Ay, you and the Gamie's unco thrang. (GAMEKEEPER *looks after them and grins*).

H.-KEEPER—Weel, than, I'll speak to onybody I like, and as lang's I like. (*Moving on*) And that's you tell't, Peter.

PETER—(*also moving on*) Ay, but ye're gey snappy fin ye see me haudin' a wark wi' Annie Simpson, maybe.

H.-KEEPER—(*scornfully, as they disappear*) Annie Simpson! Weel!

Exeunt both.

Enter LAIRD, *carrying gun.*

LAIRD—Good-day, Mr Sangster.

MAINS—Good-day, Sir Jeems.

Harvesters prepare to resume work, sharpening scythes, etc.

LAIRD—(*moving about*) You're well through with your reaping, I see.

MAINS—Ay, we'll weer throw by-and-by, maybe—wi' a push, like.

Enter PETER.

LAIRD—Well, you've had magnificent weather, and there is every indication that it is to continue.

MAINS—Jist middlin' as yet, Sir Jeems; and it's like to be waur, I doot.

PETER *makes faces.*

LAIRD—Well, you seem to have a grand crop at anyrate.

MAINS—(*stroking his chin*) Oh, jist middlin', Sir Jeems, vera middlin'.

PETER—(*aside*) Jist hearken to Mains!

LAIRD—Indeed; I thought it looked exceptionally good, and that you would be able to stand an advance in rent.

MAINS—Mercy on's a', and me sairiously thinkin' o' applyin' for a reduction.

PETER—(*aside*) What a conscience!

LAIRD—Well, how many quarters might you have to the acre here?—Six?

MAINS—Michty me, Laird! Nae muckle mair than the half o' that!—A 'owre, like, ye ken.

PETER—(aside) Isn't that awfu', boys?

LAIRD—But then corn is fetching a high figure.

MAINS—O weel, it's maybe fair eneuch the noo; but it'll be awfu' doon afore we get thrashen oot—awfu' doon!

PETER—(aside) Fegs, that cowes a'thing!

LAIRD—Indeed, indeed. I am quite astonished to find myself so far astray in my opinions and calculations.

MAINS—Ah weel, ye see, Sir Jeems, a body needs to fairm themsel's to ken richt aboot it.

LAIRD—Well, I trust you will be able at least to meet all your obligations.

MAINS—O weel, we'll maybe manage that—wi' a tchav, like.

LAIRD—And give your hands here a Harvest Home? I'm sure they deserve it.

MAINS—Weel, I wis maybe thinkin' o' that—that's to say, if things turn oot onything weel.

LAIRD—And might I make bold to look in on your festivities when the occasion comes? You know, I have never seen a Harvest Home, and should so much like to.

MAINS—I'm sure, Sir Jeems, we'll be a' greatly honoured and delighted, I'm sure.

LAIRD—Thank you, Mr Sangster.—Well, good-day.

MAINS—Good-day, Sir Jeems.

Exeunt LAIRD *and* GAMEKEEPER.

(*To* PETER) Fat sorra's he aifter wantin' to come to ony o' oor splores? To spy ferlies?

PETER—Na, he'll be gaun to stan' for Parliament, ye'll see.

MAINS—Dyod, ye're maybe richt, Peter. Weel, weel . . It'll be a great affair at onyrate. For rizzons o' my ain I want it to be the grandest splore ever seen at Mains o' Bungry. The Dominie—he's a great man for play-ackin' kin' o' things,—weel he's gettin' up something speecial for the great occasion—some kin' o' an exhibition, ye ken. Ye'll a' see't fin the time comes.— Ay, it'll be a famous splore! . . . . (*Aside, as he walks off*) For Maggie will be mine. That's the nicht I claim her. (*Exit*).

HARVESTER—(*to* PETER) Fat's up wi' the maister, Peter?

PETER—Oh, jist a maggot.

HARVESTER—And fat is the maggot?

PETER—Oh, jist Maggie and a 't' at the tail o't. Mains is gettin' Maggie, and we're gettin' the tea.—But keep your thoom on't meantime, and lat's be pushin' on.

Exeunt.

[END OF SCENE III.]

SCENE IV.—MAINS OF BUNGRY. HARVEST HOME. NIGHT.

Room with arrangements for ceremonies. Housekeeper *putting finishing touches.*

Enter Mains.

Mains—Ay, Jessie, ye've a'thing aboot richt noo?

H.-Keeper—Weel, I hope it is, Mains; we've deen oor best wi't at onyrate.

Mains—Nae doot. And noo ye'll maybe get the company brocht ben. I'll bide here and receive them as heid o' the hoose—sic heid's I am. But we'll maybe get a better ane afore vera lang.

H.-Keeper—Oh?

Mains—Ay, Jessie, I may mention there's like to be some big cheenges at Mains o' Bungry.

H.-Keeper.—Some o's will easy look aifter oorsel's whatever happens.

Mains—Noo, lassie, dinna pick a body up afore they fa'. I hid something in my e'e that I could maybe get cairret oot if—weel, if a' pairties were agreeable, like. Is Peter and you aye—weel—aye stickin' in, ye ken?

H.-Keeper—Dinna bother's, Mains!

Mains—I'm nae spierin for ill-fashions. I hiv something in my e'e, if Peter and you, ye ken could—ah weel, come to some kin' o' oonerstandin', like, ye see.

H.-Keeper—Ah weel, there's waur folk than Peter,—but,—ye see——

Mains—I've seen a' that I want to see. (*Waving her off*) Ye jist fess the folk ben.

Exit Housekeeper.

The great nicht has come! It has come and nae Shepherd. I kent he wis deid and could never come back; and noo Maggie sees't for hersel'. . . . This nicht I claim her; and she'll be mine!

Enter Company.

Welcome, friends, ane and a'—welcome to Mains o' Bungry and the Harvest Home!—And noo for the rest o' the programme.—Supper's laid oot in the Barn, and will be ready, Jessie says, aboot nine o'clock; and aifter that we'll hae a dance. Here and noo we're to be favoured wi' a kin' o' an exhibition. Mr Thomson his been good enough to get it up for the occasion, and he ca's't, I think, the Procession o' the Seasons. Sae, if a'thing's ready, Mr Thomson, ye micht jist ca' awa'.

PROCESSION OF THE SEASONS.

[As per Musical Score.]

Chorus—"TIME."

Advance, O Time, advance,
  All on thy kingly way!
Benign on us, oh, shed thy glance;
  Thy royal boon we pray.

Ascend thy throne, ascend,
  Crowned with the circling years!
Let seasons thy behest attend,
  While move the rolling spheres.

Solo and Chorus—"SPRING."

Lo, appears the happy Spring,
  Tripping fair and free,
Through the sounding woodland aisles,
  O'er the daisied lea.

    Hail, happy Spring,
    Happy, happy Spring!

Solo and Chorus—"SUMMER."

With stately pace and matron grace
  The Summer moves along;
Around her blows June's living rose,
  And airs of noontide throng.

Season of light and song,
  Blossom and balmy gale,
Fondly awaited and long,
  Glorious Summer, hail!
    Hail, hail, hail!

Solo and Chorus—"AUTUMN."

Through orchards rosy-hued and golden fields,
  Fair Autumn's wide demesne,
Laden with all the bounteous season yields,
  Behold the Harvest Queen!
    Hail, hail, hail!
    Hail to the Harvest Queen!

Chorus and Dance—"THE HOURS."

Merry, merry maidens,
  Maidens fair and sweet,
Whence, oh tell us, and whither,
  Roam your happy feet.

O'er the breezy moorland,
  Gleaming with golden whin;
Down where blooms of the valley
  Dip to the laughing linn;
Through the fairy woodland,
  Shadowed with green of May,
Where the mavis is singing
  All the summer day.

Merry, merry maidens,
  Maidens sweet and fair,
Tell us what ye have gathered,
  Whose the spoils ye bear.

Daffodil, daisy, and primrose,
  Gathered by burn and brae;
Rose, and lily, and pansy,
  From many a garden gay;
Spoils of the Springtime and Summer,
  Culled in each fairy scene,—
These the gifts that we offer,
  All to our Harvest Queen

Chorus—"LORD OF THE SEASONS."

Lord of the Seasons, Thou art good;
  God of the years, in Thee we live;
Firm has Thy gracious covenant stood;
  Seed-time and harvest Thou dost give.

Lo, from Thy hand, the golden year
  Comes with Thy goodness richly crowned;
So may our songs of grateful cheer
  High to Thy Heavenly Throne resound!

MAINS—Weel, that's fell bonnie, noo.   I'm sure we've a'
enjoyed the thing: and we're muckle indebted to a' the bonnie
lasses, and lads, tee, that hae ta'en pairt in't, and likewise Mr
Thomson for his trouble in gettin't up.   Lat's gie them three
cheers.

Company cheer.

Fiddle heard without playing "Bonnie Lass o' Bon-Accord."

Company listen.

DOMINIE—(*excited*) Good Heavens!   What can that be?
MAINS—Oh, jist some chiel or ither playin' the furth—fat ither?
Likely eneuch it's some o' oor fiddlers come owre seen.   He'll
be haein' a bit practice till himsel'.

DOMINIE—No—really—I don't think it can be that. . . . .
In any case mightn't we bring him in? He seems a good hand,
and should be worth his room.

MAINS—O surely: we canna hae owre muckle meesic.—Peter,
gang and bring the chiel in.

DOMINIE—No, I'll go myself, if you'll excuse me. (*Exit*).

MAINS—The Dominie's in an awfu' pichertie aboot that fiddler.

SOUTER—He's some nervish kin' the Dominie. Ye min' yon
time at the picnic, fin he wis proposin' a vote o' thanks to the
Laird?

MAINS—Ay; and speakin' o' the Laird min's me that he'll
maybe be lookin' in on's the nicht. Sae dinna be astonished if
he come stumpin' in; but gin he dee, we'll a' need to min' oor
p's and q's, boys.

PETER—Oh, we'll fairly dee that.

Enter DOMINIE *with* SHEPHERD *in old disguise, but
without markings on face.*

DOMINIE—(*leading him forward*) Here is our man. He seems
to be a wandering minstrel, and almost blind; and he would like
a night's quarters if possible.

MAINS—He'll easy get that, and a guid supper forbye; but
he'll hae to gie's a spring for't. Jist lat's hear yon teen again ye
wis playin' the furth wi' the variations

SHEPHERD—With pleasure, sir. (*Plays tune*).

MAINS—Thank ye, that's fine. And hae ye onything mair o'
the same kind?

DOMINIE—Excuse me, Mr Sangster, but these hereditary
minstrels have frequently the gift of second sight. Perhaps this
old man can read fortunes. It might prove an interesting diver-
sion for our younger friends.

MAINS—That's a good idea.

SOUTER—(*nudging* JEANNIE) Oh fairly.

MAINS—Weel, Fiddly, can ye dee onything in the wizard line?

SHEPHERD—Yes, I have that gift; and if any maiden here
will give me her hand I will do my best to let her know what
fortune has in store for her.

MAINS—Capital! Come, some o' you lassies! The mannie
here will tell ye a' aboot the chaps ye're to get—whether your
man's to be bow-hocht, or skyow-fittet, reid-heidet, or squint-e'ed;
whether he's to be a dominie, a darger, or a pigman, or a big
fairmer like me wi' a guid quyte on his back and plenty siller
in's pouch.

SOUTER—Or a fine-lookin' Souter like me.

PETER—(*grinning*) Weel, weel! (*To* JEANNIE) Ye'll be gey
prood, Jeannie.

SOUTER—Or a peer breet like Peter here. (*To* HOUSEKEEPER)
Eh, Jessie lass?

MAINS—That'll dee, boys. (*To* SHEPHERD) Ye can tell them a that, canna ye, Fiddly?

SHEPHERD—Well, that's rather a big order; but I can at least tell them something about their love affairs.

DOMINIE—(*who has been whispering to* MAGGIE, *coming forward*) Very good.—Suppose we ask him to begin with the Harvest Queen?

MAINS—A fine beginnin'. And aifter that he can tak' (*looking round*)—ah, weel say—Maggie Anderson.

> DOMINIE *leads forward* HARVEST QUEEN. SHEPHERD *takes her hand and bends over it for a little.*

> *Chants (with soft accompaniment)—*

Key G.

$$\left\{ \begin{array}{l} \| \textbf{d . d,d : d . d} \quad | \quad \textbf{d} \quad : — . \textbf{d} \quad | \quad \textbf{d . d : d.,s}_| \quad | \quad \textbf{s}_| \quad : \\ \| \text{Maid, with the [golden] hair, And} \quad | \quad \text{cheeks so fresh and fair,} \end{array} \right.$$

$$\left\{ \begin{array}{l} | \textbf{d . d,d : d . d} \quad | \quad \textbf{d.,s}_| : \textbf{s}_{|.}, \textbf{s}_| \quad | \quad \textbf{s}_| \textbf{. s}_| : \textbf{l}_{|.}, \textbf{s}_| \quad | \quad \textbf{s}_| : — \\ | \text{Strange are the tangled threads of love the fates now spin for} \quad \text{thee—} \end{array} \right.$$

$$\left\{ \begin{array}{l} | \textbf{d . d,d : d . d} \quad | \quad \textbf{d} \quad : — .\textbf{d} \quad | \quad \textbf{d . d : d., s}_| \quad | \quad \textbf{s}_| \quad : \\ | \text{Fond are the lovers twain} \quad \text{who} \quad | \quad \text{strive thy heart to gain;} \end{array} \right.$$

$$\left\{ \begin{array}{l} | \textbf{d . d,d : d . d} \quad | \quad \textbf{d., s : s}_. \quad \textbf{s}_| \quad | \quad \textbf{s}_| \textbf{. s}_| : \textbf{l}_{|.}, \textbf{s}_| \quad | \quad \textbf{s}_| : — \| \\ | \text{Yet shall a third the} \quad \text{victor prove, and} \quad | \quad \text{take thee o'er the sea.} \| \end{array} \right.$$

MAINS—(*to* HARVEST QUEEN) Ay, ay, Your Majesty, and that's a gey revelation, maybe. *Ye'll* be a' richt at onyrate, although we're some sorry for the twa chaps that ye're to leave ahin'. Ye couldna weel hae ta'en them baith, hooever, and this 'ill stop their fechtin'.—Weel, weel. (*To* MAGGIE) It's your turn, noo, Maggie. (*To* SHEPHERD) And min', Fiddly, ye'll need to be on your mettle this time—min' that.

DOMINIE—(*leading* MAGGIE *forward*) Yes, now's your chance.

SHEPHERD—I shall do my best, and I hope it may please all parties.

MAINS—Nae fear o' that, gin it be the truth.

SHEPHERD—It *will* be the truth. Depend on that!

SHEPHERD *takes* MAGGIE'S *hand, and bends over it for a little.*

Chants, as before—

Maid, with the [auburn] hair,
And eyes so deep and rare,
Now is love's web for thee complete, its last fair
thread is spun—
Of lovers twain the dearest
Stands at this moment nearest,
To claim this night his guerdon sweet—the heart
that he has won.

MAINS—GRAND! Man, Fiddly, ye *are* a wizard, gin ever there *wis* ane! Ye've fairly strucken the nail on the heid *this* time. For (*striking an attitude, tapping himself on the breast, and imitating* SHEPHERD'S *chant*)—

He's here, he's here, he's he—re,
The very very man is ne—ar,
To claim this night his—his—

(*Spoken*) Ach!—Jist his Lass! (*Advancing and offering to take her hand*)—Maggie!

SHEPHERD *waves* MAINS *aside. Taps himself on the breast, and chants, as before—*

Nay, nay, he's here that's dearer,
The very very man is nearer,
To claim this night (*putting his arm round* MAGGIE)—

MAINS—(*interrupting with sudden fury*) Ye auld blagaird! Fat dee ye mean? Come oot o' that! (*Seizing* SHEPHERD *by the arm*) Hoo daur ye lay hands on my lass?

SHEPHERD—She is mine.

MAINS—Yours, ye auld blagaird!—She's MINE!

They struggle for possession of MAGGIE. MAINS *at length seizes* SHEPHERD *by beard. It comes off in his hand. He looks at it in horror and disgust; then flings it on floor.* SHEPHERD *swiftly casts off the rest of his disguise, and stands revealed. He puts his arm again round* MAGGIE, *who leans her head on his shoulder.* MAINS *throws up his hands in dismay, and, uttering a cry of astonishment, staggers backward, and collapses into a chair.*

Company, who laugh merrily during the encounter between MAINS *and* SHEPHERD, *throw up their hands with* MAINS, *and join in his cry.*

PETER *runs to* MAINS'S *side, and pats him on the back.*

Mrs A.—(*coming hastily forward*) O Mr Sangster!

PETER—(*shaking his fist at the* SHEPHERD) Will I kill him, Mains?

MAINS—(*speaking in gasps*) Na, Peter—ye canna, min.—He's a corp! There's a stane gaun up till 'im in the kirkyaird. He's gaun wrang—fest. His whiskers cam oot—awfu' easy.

PETER—Corp! Fient a bit o' 'im. Jist look at the whiskers! (*Shows them*)—And look at him (*pointing*). Ye never saw a corp winkin', min.

MAINS—Weel, than—he's a ghost!

PETER—Haivers, min! Ye never saw a lassie wi' her heid on a ghost's shouther, min!

MAINS—Ye're sure he's livin'?

SHEPHERD—Ay, Mains, here I am alive and well, and glad to be back again among you all.

MAINS—Weel, weel, fa wid hae thocht it? Cowes a' green thing, min! (*Blows his nose, wipes his eyes, etc.*) Noo, Peter, man, help me on till my legs. (PETER *helps him to his feet*). Noo, haud's a meenit, will ye?—like a man, till I get steady. (*Steadying himself*) That'll dee, Peter, my man. Ye're nae an ill breet ava. Noo stand ootbye. I'm gaun to mak' a speech— maybe my hinmost ane; and I wid like to rise to the occasion. (*Hums and haws in preparation. Addressing* SHEPHERD *who, with* MAGGIE, *has remained in original position*) John Murison, shepherd, sodger, corp, kirkyaird deserter, fiddler, wizard, and shepherd ance mair—listen!

PETER—Jock Meerison! Listen!

MAINS—(*waving* PETER *aside*) Weesht, Peter min, I'll manage him mysel'! . . . . John Murison, lang hae you and I been rivals; lang has been the battle atween's. Only a moment ago I flattered mysel' that Fate had gien me the victory, and that to-night I would claim Maggie as my ain. But, at the very moment o' my supposed triumph, ye appear as fae the deid, to snatch the prize fae my hands. Such is life, such is fate. Sae be it! Ye hae won, and I yield. (*Advancing and taking* MAGGIE'S *hand*) Tak' her. (*Putting her hand into* SHEPHERD'S) Tak' her wi' my blessin'; for do not I now know how bravely once you adventured your life in defence of mine? And, to show my gratitude and goodwill, I shall settle you in Knoweheid, and thus enable you to retain the old place for Maggie and her widowed mother.

SHEPHERD—(*seizing* MAINS'S *hand*) Mains! Noble, generous soul, how can we thank you?

MAINS—Weesht, min; nae anither word, see! (*Wiping his eyes with big red handkerchief*).

MAGGIE—O Mains!

Mrs A.—O Mr Sangster!

MAINS—It's a' richt! God bless ye a'! (*Wiping his eyes and blowing his nose*).

Mrs A.—But what aboot your poor sel', Mr Sangster?

MAINS—Oh, never mind me.   I'll jist hae to continue my auld bachelor life.   There's naething else for me noo.

Mrs A.—O Mr Sangster!

PETER—Buff and nonsense, min! Ye're nae needin' to dee that unless it be for thrawnness.

MAINS—Fat d'ye mean, Peter min?

PETER—Weel, there's nae eese o' bidin' an auld bachelor as lang's there's a guid, dacent, sensible 'umman o' yer ain age, willin' to tak ye.

MAINS—Peter, min! Fat d'ye mean, min?

PETER—Canna ye see't yersel', min? Ye're unco blin'. (*Inclining his head towards* Mrs A.).

MAINS—(*turning eagerly to* Mrs A.) Is't you, Mrs Anderson? Will *ye* hae me? Come noo, will ye hae me yersel'?

Mrs A.—(*simpering*) O Mr Sangster!

MAINS—Come noo, say ay or no!

Mrs A.—O Mr Sangster, this is so sudden.

MAINS—Never min' that! A'thing's been suddent the nicht. We can tak' mair time to things aifterhin.

Mrs A.—This is so unexpected.—And then there's the memory o' poor John Anderson, you know.

MAINS—Oh, jist lat John Anderson lie! He wis a dacent eneuch auld carle; but he's awa', and I'm here; and as the Scriptur says, A deid dog is better than a livin' lion.

SOUTER—Hoot awa', Mains! Ye mean, a livin' lion is better than a deid dog.

DOMINIE—Excuse me, gentlemen, but you're both wrong. The passage runs, A living dog is better than a dead lion. You will find it in, I think, Ecclesiastes, if you had a bible——

MAINS—(*exasperated*) Haud your lang tongues, ye twa bletherin' idiots! Ye'll pit a man mad! (*Turning to* Mrs A.) Mrs Anderson—Maggie, will ye hae me? Answer me that!

Mrs A.—O Mr Sangster, what can I say?

SOUTER—Mains, man, ye seerly dinna ken the wyes o' women folk.   Dinna ye see she's takin' ye?

MAINS—Foo disn' she say't than?

SOUTER—Man, women never gie a chap a straucht-oot answer. For instance, fin I socht Jeannie here——

JEANNIE—(*slapping him on the cheek*) Haud yer tongue, Willie!

MAINS—Weel, than, Maggie, it's a' richt? Ye're takin' me?

Mrs A.—O Mains!

MAINS—Yer hand on't! (*She gives her hand*).

Company cheer.

DOMINIE—(*coming forward*) In name of this festive company, allow me to offer the parties concerned our warmest congratulations on the happy and auspicious termination of this most exciting and singularly interesting episode. Our sincere felicitations for the present, and our best wishes for the future. (*Shakes hands with* SHEPHERD *and* MAGGIE, *and then with* MAINS *and* Mrs A.).

SHEPHERD—Thank you, Mr Thomson   Thank you, kind friends, one and all.

MAINS—Mony thanks to ye a'!—Weel than, *that's a' richt.* (*Turning to* PETER) Noo Peter, my man, ye've deen lots o' jobbies for me, and this hinmost ane's been the best. I'm gaun to tak' you in han' noo.

PETER—Yea?

MAINS—Ay.—Weel, ye see, fin I get mairriet, I mean to rise to the dignity o' my new position, and ack the gentleman fairmer, ye ken. I'll maybe wear a fite lum-hat, fa' kens, and speak English. Noo, to cairry oot my idea, I maun hae a kin' o' a grieve and general manager aboot the toon. I'll gie him guid wages; but he maun be a mairriet man, and tak' up hoose.— Noo, Peter, will ye tak' the job?

PETER—But ye ken fine, Mains, I'm single.

MAINS—Fat's the eese o' ye bidin' single as lang's there's a dacent, sensible 'umman o' yer ain age, willin' to tak' ye?

PETER—Mains, min, fat are ye drivin' at?

MAINS—Canna ye see't yersel', min?   Ye're unco blin'! (*Inclining his head towards* HOUSEKEEPER).

PETER—Oh, I see fat ye're aifter.   But she maybe winna hae me.

MAINS—Hae ye socht her?

PETER—Weel—nae jist yet at onyrate.

MAINS—(*to* HOUSEKEEPER) Come here, Jessie. (*She approaches.* To PETER) Noo, seek her. I ken she'll tak' ye, for she tell't me hersel' the nicht already.

H.-KEEPER—Mains!

MAINS—Ach! gie him yer hand, Jessie, and nae mair aboot it!—We're deein' things suddenter ilka time the nicht. (*She gives* PETER *her hand*). Noo, that's a' richt. Ye'll be my manager, Peter; and Jessie'll be yours.

Knock.

But rin, Peter, man. There's surely mair company comin'.

Exit PETER. *Re-enter with* SERGEANT *and* POLICEMAN.

SERGEANT—Excuse me, sir; I am sorry to intrude.

MAINS—Oh, nae intrusion ava. We're rale gled to see twa sic braw chaps, and ye couldna hae come handier gin ye want to enjoy yersel's.

SERGEANT—But I fear I come on a disagreeable errand, to one of the company at least. (*Looking towards* SHEPHERD, *who has been showing signs of great alarm, and trying to get in behind some of the company*).

Mains—Oh, that's a pity. Fat's adee?

Sergeant—(to Shepherd) Come forward, sir. (Shepherd comes into view). This man here, John Mackay, is a deserter.

Mains—Oh, ye're fairly wrang, man. That chiel's ca'd John Murison.

Sergeant—That may be; but we knew him as Private John Mackay of the 95th Regiment, from which he has now deserted.

Mains—But hoo did ye manage to trace him? Man,—the rig he wis in—I widna kent him amo' my porridge.

Sergeant—Everyone to his trade. Anyhow we have caught our man.

Shepherd—Sergeant, I didn't desert. I only came home to—to——

Mains—To see his lass, of coorse.

Sergeant—That is no plea.

Mains—Hid ye ever a lass yersel', Sergeant?

Sergeant—Perhaps I have.

Mains—And canna ye understand a chap wha hisna seen his ain true love for a year and a day wantin' hame to get a look o' her bonnie face, and hear ance mair fae her sweet lips that she's aye true to him?

Sergeant—That's sentiment, not discipline. The man is a deserter.

Dominie—Excuse me, Sergeant, is that the case? He may have come away without leave of absence. That is a military offence, certainly, but I fail to see how it can be construed as desertion.

Sergeant—I haven't time to bandy words. Private, you accompany me back to headquarters at once.

Shepherd—O me; I'm clean gone! (Maggie clings to him). And to leave you, Maggie, and maybe never get back!

Maggie—Go, Johnnie, if it's your duty to go; and I'll wait for you—years if you like!

Mains—I say, Sergeant, fat wid it tak' to buy this man aff?

Sergeant—Twenty pounds, sir. But meantime he is a deserter.

Mains—Oh, jist gie that stringie a rest. Ye've tittet it lang eneuch. Kennin' a' the circumstances o' the case, ye can easy pit a guid face on that bit o't. (Takes out his pocket-book).

Shepherd—O Mains, what do you mean?

Mains—Never ye mind, Shepherd. (Taking out notes) Wi' this twa-three notes I wis gaun to pit up a stane till ye in the kirkyaird; but, bein' a restless kin' o' a chiel, ye widna bide deid lang eneuch, and so noo I'll jist hae to spend the siller on ye livin'. (To Sergeant) Here's fower guid fivers. (Sergeant hesitates to take the money). Tak' it, man. It's guid siller. Ye're a brave man, and the brave are aye the maist mercifu'.

Sergeant—Well, I should like to oblige, but——

MAINS—Nae buts aboot it.   Here !   (*Puts notes into* SER-
GEANT'S hand. *Takes a scrap of paper and writes on it*). Noo,
jist ye sign that I.O.U. That'll dee meantime ; and ye can mak'
oot a' the necessar' papers aifterwards. (SERGEANT *signs paper,
and hands back to* MAINS). Man, ye're a brick, and here's something for a dram to you and the Bobby. (*Hands him a pound
note*).   And, gin ye're nae in an awfu' hurry, ye can baith
bide and hae some fun.
     SHEPHERD—O Mains, what can I say ?
     MAGGIE—O Mains, what can we say ?
     MAINS—Jist haud your tongues, baith o' ye, and say naething
ava !
                    Knock, and enter LAIRD.

Oh, come awa', Sir Jeems, come awa' !—Awfu' things been
happenin' here the nicht !
     LAIRD—Indeed ; and what has occurred ?
     MAINS—Oh, I could never tell ye the half o't. It's jist been
like a saxpenny novel. (*Striking an attitude*) But, first and
foremost, I'm to be mairriet mysel' !
     LAIRD—Very good, very good, Mr Sangster. I am delighted
to hear it. And who is to be the——·
     MAINS—Fortunate woman ? It's Mrs Anderson here. (*Leads
her forward*).
     LAIRD—Oh, very good indeed ; a delightful arrangement.
Allow me to congratulate you both. (*Shakes hands with* Mrs A.
and MAINS).
     MAINS—Ay, and there's mair matches, Sir Jeems. Shepherd,
stand forth, and Maggie Anderson. (*They come forward*).
     LAIRD—Oh ! Our old friend, the Shepherd ! I'm glad, sir,
to see you back among us once more, not only with your name
cleared, but with your reputation as a brave man very greatly
enhanced.
     SHEPHERD—(*saluting*) Thank you, Sir James.
     MAINS—That's sae, Sir Jeems. Weel, Maggie Anderson and
the Shepherd's gaun to be mairriet. Atween you and me, Sir
Jeems, I ance thocht I micht get Maggie mysel' ; but ye see she's
ta'en the Shepherd, and that's the wye that I fell back on her
mither, ye ken.
     LAIRD—A most sensible thing to do, Mr Sangster.
     Mrs A.—(*curtseying*) Thank you, Sir James.
     MAINS—Ay, but fa' kens ?—gin the Shepherd and his guid-
mither wis baith to dee, I micht get a chance o' Maggie aiftern a'.
     Mrs A.—Mains !
     LAIRD—Never mind, Mrs Anderson ; there are too many if's
in the matter, not to speak of the legal difficulties.
     MAINS—Dyod, I didna think o' that noo. I suppose than I'll
jist need to be content wi' my ain auld woman. (*Starting as* Mrs
A. *pinches his arm*) Aliss ! (*Rubs arm*).—Weel, as I wis sayin',

the twa's to be mairriet. They'll cairry on the lease at Knowe-heid, gin it's agreeable to you, Sir Jeems, and I'll stand guid for a'thing.

LAIRD—Very good, Mr Sangster; that's all right. A very nice arrangement indeed, and I congratulate the young people.

MAINS—Noo, Souter and Jeannie, stand forth. This is the twa that we took Waulkie's place for.

LAIRD—Very good.

MAINS—And last o' a', there's my man Peter, wha's to mairry the hoosekeeper, and be my grieve.

LAIRD—These arrangements are all most excellent, Mr Sangster. You've had quite a matrimonial market. But (*looking round Company*) have you left any single people at all?

MAINS—Ah weel, ane or twa maybe—jist for the look o' the thing, ye ken. But we'll work them aff neist time.

And noo, kin' freens, ane and a', I promised ye a splore the nicht; and it *his* been a splore—bigger than I bargained for, and a gey bittie awa' fae the programme. But it's a' weel that ends weel. The neist great event will be a fower-fald waddin'—fat the history books wid ca' a Quadruple Alliance. And I think we'll hae't at Yule, if that's agreeable to a' concerned. And the ane or twa o' ye here that's nae to be mairriet yersels ye're hertily inveetit to be present and see hiz folk pitten throw the mull. Ye'll mind that?

And noo lat's bring the proceedin's o' this momentous occasion till a fittin' close by a' joinin' in Auld Lang Syne. (*Company sing Auld Lang Syne.* MAINS *advances to front*). And that's the end o' Mains's Wooin'?—Weel, weel!

[THE END.]

Return to

Mains's Wooin'

Piano.

G. Greig
New D.

Hame and Guid-nicht. Cho.

Heavenly Power. – Trio.

Sleep, my own – Solo.

Sleep my own, my loved one, Angels guard thee now....

Bless thy dreaming sper - it Crown with peace thy brow....

Hear my prayer High Heav - en In this anguished hour......

In Thy mercy shield - - him Save him by Thy power.

rall. e. dim.

Duet. Fare-thee-well.

(To same accompaniment as "Sleep my own").

(Solo. Shepherd) ... Fare thee well, my own one,
Parting here in pain.
Knowing not if ever
We may meet again. -

(Duet.) Hear our vow, High Heaven
Mark our plighted faith,
Changeless, unforgetting,
We are true till death.

(Solo - Maggie) Summertide and winter,
All the coming years,
Still in sun and shadow,
Still 'mid smiles and tears,

(Duet.) Love, and faith undying
In this breast shall dwell,
Heart-enshrined for ever.
Darling, fare thee well.

Guid-nicht and joy. Solo & Cho.

Lads and Lasses. — Cho & Solo.

The bonnie Lass o' Fyvie - Solo.

Vivace

There was a troop o' Irish dragoons, cam marchin' up thro' Fyvie O.

And the Captain's fain in love wi' a very bonnie lass and her name 'tis called pretty Peggie O.

It's oh for the good old days - Solo.

Johnnie Sangster – Solo & Cho.

O' a' the seasons o' the year When we maun work the sairest. The

harvest is the foremost time + yet it is the sairest. We rise as soon as mornin leafs The cruidies can be blither. We

buckle on oor finger steels + follow oot the scythe. For you Johnnie you Johnnie you Johnnie Sangster, I'll

trim the gavel o' my sheaf for ye're the gallant bandster.

Lord of the Seasons. Cho.

Lord of the seasons thou art good
So from Thy hand the golden year
God of the years in thee we live
Time with Thy goodness richly crowned

Firm has Thy gracious covenant stood
So may our songs of grateful cheer
Seed time & harvest
With Thy heavenly showers give
throne resound

no accompt

Fortune - telling - Solo.

Maid with the —— cheeks ——
Find on the —— brow ——
Strange ——
Yet what
fates —— than
take —— sea.

Auld Lang Syne.

The End.

Mama's "Wooin'" Selection

Gavin Greig.

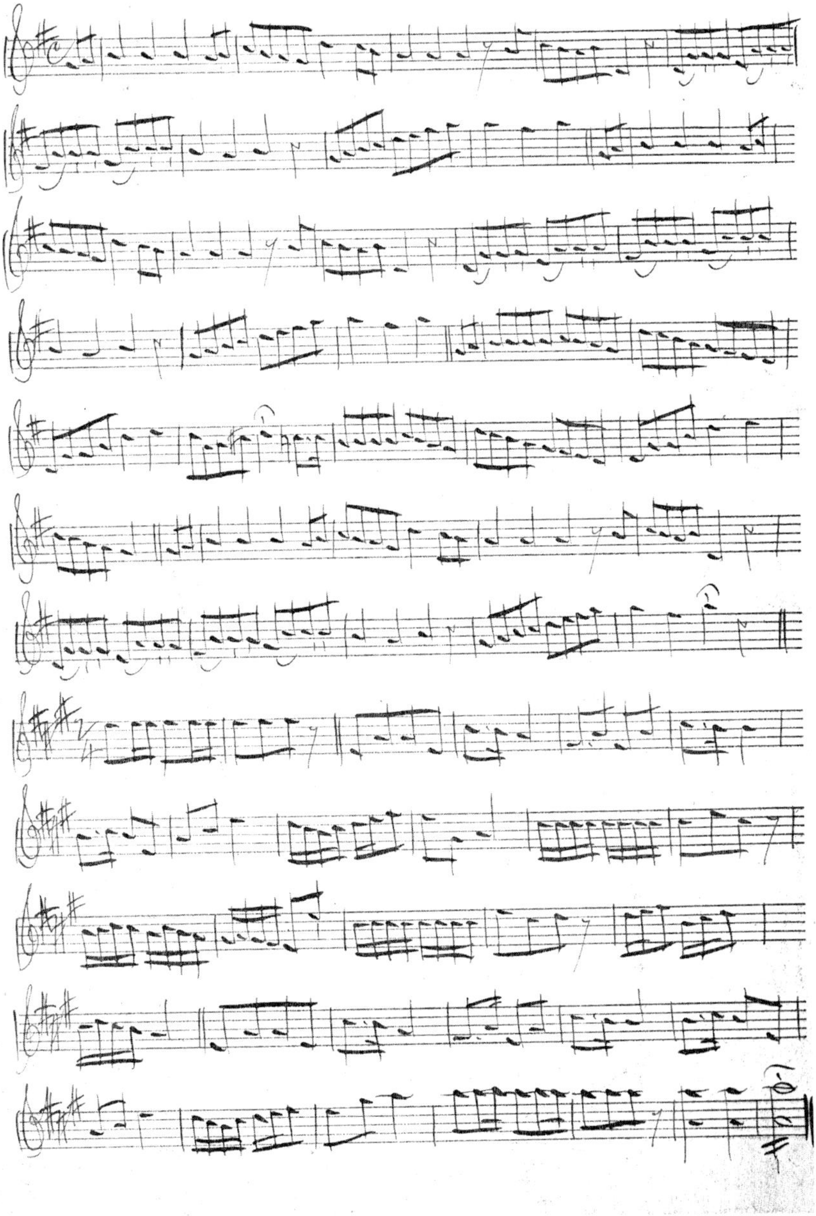